Penguin Edu

Penguin Englis
Edited by Albert Levine

WEST WYTHENSHAWE
COLLEGE of FE
Moor Road
Wythenshawe Manchester M23 9BQ

Penguin
English Reader

Edited by Albert Levine

Penguin Books

Penguin Books Ltd, Harmondsworth, Middlesex, England
Penguin Books Australia Ltd, Ringwood, Victoria, Australia

First published 1971
This selection copyright © Albert Levine, 1971

Made and printed in Great Britain
by Hazell Watson & Viney Ltd
Aylesbury, Bucks
Set in Monotype Plantin

This book is sold subject to the condition
that it shall not, by way of trade or otherwise,
be lent, re-sold, hired out, or otherwise circulated
without the publisher's prior consent in any form of
binding or cover other than that in which it is
published and without a similar condition
including this condition being imposed
on the subsequent purchaser

Preface

This collection of passages for the advanced student of English as a foreign language has been drawn from the widest possible range of sources to illustrate the kind of English that average English people read in their spare time, and the signs, notices, advertisements, warnings and instructions that they absorb every day.

This is the language of contemporary Britain, literary and technical, popular and traditional. It ranges from the entertaining to the extraordinary, but is always representative of today. The advanced student may use this book for bedside reading, on train journeys, for simply dipping into, or for classroom work and discussion. The passages are not arranged in order of difficulty, but are juxtaposed to provide variety and contrast.

Glosses are given on vocabulary which is not easily found in *The Advanced Learners' Dictionary of Current English* by A. S. Hornby, E. V. Gatenby and H. Wakefield (Oxford University Press), and explanatory notes are given where the social or cultural references may be unfamiliar.

This preface would not be complete without recording my grateful thanks to the members of my family who did so much of the donkey work, to Philip W. Lawrence for his generous scholarship, and to Nora Levine who took endless trouble with the manuscript.

Guide to Metric Equivalents of English Weights and Measures Mentioned in the Text

Length

1 inch (in) = 2·54 centimetres
1 foot (ft) = 0·3048 metre
1 yard (yd) = 0·9144 metre

Area

1 acre (4840 sq. yd) = 0·405 hectare
1 square inch (sq. in) = 6·4516 square centimetres

Capacity

1 pint (pt) = 0·568 litre

Weight

1 ounce (oz) = 28·35 grammes
1 pound (lb) = 0·454 kilogramme
1 stone (st) = 6·350 kilogrammes

Thermometer scales

Boiling point: 212° Farenheit = 100° Centigrade
Freezing point: 32° Farenheit = 0° Centigrade

1

This Scepter'd Three-Fifths

Sir,

In this week's issue of the *Observer*, John Crosby refers to England as an island.

Is it possible to have this matter settled once and for all – at least so far as the *Observer* is concerned? 5

England is *not* an island. She is only three-fifths of an island.

Ronald MacDonald-Douglas
The 1320 Club, Hawick, Scotland

John Crosby writes: This gentleman seems to think an 10 island must be surrounded by water. England is an island as Rhode Island is an island, as Piccadilly Circus is an island, as no man is an island.

Letter in the *Observer*, 14 September 1969

Title *This Scepter'd Three-Fifths:* a deliberate misquotation from Shakespeare's *Richard II*, Act 2 Scene 1: '. . . this scepter'd isle/This earth of majesty . . .'

2 the *Observer:* a quality Sunday newspaper.

13 *no man is an island:* a quotation from a sermon by John Donne: 'no man is an island entire unto himself'.

2

If you are thinking of spending your money on something 1 to put into your mouth which is supposed to slim you without any need for you to control your eating, you must ask two questions. First, is this going to make you use up your food quicker? If so, it is likely to be thyroid hormone or 5 some similar substance, and should on no account be taken without asking your doctor. Second, is it going to make you stick to a slimming diet more easily? If so, make sure first you have got the best possible advice about the diet itself.

Apart from food and drinks, there are other nonsense 10 recommendations for slimming. One is that you should take Turkish baths, or some similar and probably more costly way of sweating hard. I have already explained that you will of course lose weight while you are undergoing this treatment. You learn in school that a pint of water weighs a pound and a quarter, and it is quite easy to lose a pint by sweating. And it is just as easy to put this pint back into your dehydrated tissues as soon as you begin to drink again. One of the more amusing variants of this game is to wear some sort of rubber or plastic garment for a time. The effect is much the same, a temporary loss of weight through dehydration.

What about massage? The best way to answer this is to think of our factory once more. If you are lying quite still and being rubbed and pounded about, the chances of some of your fat disappearing are just as likely as if you tried to get rid of excessive stores of fuel in your factory by massaging the coal. Fat will not just 'dissolve'. It has to be burned up. And this will only happen if your body finds that you are being mean with the calories from your food so that it has to burn up your fat reserves. Improving the circulation in your fatty tissues will help as much as having a lot of workmen in the factory just running in and out of the fuel store. But if you insist, I shall have to agree that massage might possibly have a reducing effect – on the person who is doing the massage.

Exercises which you yourself do are a bit different. Firstly, I have already said that if you do more physical work, you will help to reduce your weight, provided that you don't make up by eating more. Secondly, some sorts of exercises will improve the tone of your muscles. This may help to reduce your shape, though not your weight.

Nevertheless if your tummy is somewhat bigger than it should be, it is possible that you will at least look better, though not weigh less, if you learn to strengthen your tummy muscles.

John Yudkin: *This Slimming Business* (MacGibbon & Kee, 1958; Penguin Books, 1962)

3

£338,000. He's Still Only Old Percy

The *luckiest* man in Britain. That's what they call Percy 1
Harrison, the only punter to have a super scoop-the-pool
win this season.

Others may have won their thousands, some their tens
of thousands, but there has been nothing to equal the 5
£338,356 16s. Percy collected last September.

And it was only the second time he'd 'done the pools'.

Well, I'm able to let you into a secret. Percy's luck is still
holding. Ever since he won all that money, Percy has been
determined not to let it change him . . . and he's done it. 10

As he loosened his wide leather belt and squeezed out of
his gumboots last week he looked just like the man he
used to be, a £13-a-week labourer with a fertilizer firm.

'Money,' he said as he talked about his fortune for the
first time since his big win, 'is worth having only as long 15
as you don't let it change your way of life.

'If you try to become somebody different you end up by
making yourself miserable.'

Simple Man

'Fancy living? You can keep your champagne and your 20
posh hotels. I'm just a plain, simple man – and that's the
way I'll always be.'

Although Percy now runs a small farm, I believe him.

It will take a lot to change this ruddy-faced Yorkshire
lad. Certainly the rich life won't do it. 25

'I don't want to go through that again for as long as I
live,' he said, referring to the ballyhoo when he went to
London to collect his cheque. 'If that's your high living
you can keep it.'

No, Percy is more at home on the land and it was at his 30
fifty-acre farm, at a village between York and Hull, that I
saw him.

Proudly he showed me a spacious barn and a fine tractor.

His eyes twinkled as he said: 'When I called at the
dealers I was dressed like I always am.' 35

Percy showed me large holes in the elbows of his old woollen pullover.

'I told the man what I wanted to buy, but he said they didn't have any secondhand tractors for sale.

40 'It was only when I showed him a fistful of fivers that he cottoned on.'

Strangely enough, the proud tractor owner doesn't run a car.

'I don't drive and I don't want to,' he said. . . .

45 But success has brought its share of worry for Mr and Mrs Harrison.

Since their mammoth win they have been plagued with an endless succession of callers and spongers.

That is why, on the entrance to the farm, is a large notice 50 painted in black and white: 'No admittance – except by prior appointment.'

Len Adams in the *People*, 25 May 1967

2 *scoop-the-pool win:* to win all the prize money.

7 '*done the pools*': filled in a coupon for the football pools, that is, placed money on the results of a series of football matches in the hope of winning the prize money.

20 *fancy living:* living in an extravagant way.

41 *cottoned on:* understood (colloquial).

48 *spongers:* people who live at someone else's expense (colloquial).

4

1 There wasn't a sound. Chester lifted his head and very cautiously looked behind him. The cat – a huge tiger cat with grey-green and black stripes along his body – was sitting on his hind legs, switching his tail around his fore-
5 paws. And directly between those forepaws, in the very jaws of the enemy, sat Tucker Mouse. He was watching Chester curiously. The cricket began to make frantic signs that the mouse should look up and see what was looming over him.

10 Very casually Tucker raised his head. The cat looked straight down on him. 'Oh him,' said Tucker, chucking

the cat under the chin with his right front paw, 'he's my best friend. Come out from the matchbox.'

Chester crept out, looking first at one, then the other.

'Chester, meet Harry Cat,' said Tucker. 'Harry, this is Chester. He's a cricket.'

'I'm very pleased to make your acquaintance,' said Harry Cat in a silky voice.

'Hello,' said Chester. He was sort of ashamed because of all the fuss he'd made. 'I wasn't scared for myself. But I thought cats and mice were enemies.'

'In the country, maybe,' said Tucker. 'But in New York we gave up those old habits long ago. Harry is my oldest friend. He lives with me over in the drainpipe. So how was scrounging tonight, Harry?'

'Not so good,' said Harry Cat. 'I was over in the ash cans on the East Side, but those rich people don't throw out as much garbage as they should.'

'Chester, make that noise again for Harry,' said Tucker Mouse.

Chester lifted the black wings that were carefully folded across his back and with a quick expert stroke drew the top one over the bottom. A 'thrumm' echoed through the station.

'Lovely – very lovely,' said the cat. 'This cricket has talent.'

'I thought it was singing,' said Tucker. 'But you do it like playing a violin, with one wing on the other?'

'Yes,' said Chester. 'These wings aren't much good for flying, but I prefer music anyhow.' He made three rapid chirps.

Tucker Mouse and Harry Cat smiled at each other. 'It makes me want to purr to hear it,' said Harry.

George Selden: *The Cricket in Times Square* (Dent, 1961; Penguin Books, 1963)

26 *ash cans:* rubbish bins (US usage).
27 *the East Side:* a district in New York.

5

José Must Wait for Winstone

1 Howard Winstone, world featherweight champion, duly signed yesterday to meet Jimmy Anderson, first holder of the newly created junior lightweight (9 st. 4 lb) title, at Wembley, on 9 April.

5 The fight will be at 9 st. 6 lb so that neither man's title will be at stake.

What of the dark shadow of José Legra, whom Winstone had agreed to meet for the world 9-stone title within ninety days of winning the vacant championship by beating the
10 Japanese Mitsunori Saki?

Said Winstone's manager, Eddie Thomas: 'I am hoping that the fight will be in the summer, either in Wales or London. We will go wherever the money is.'

Then he added that they had had an offer of £27,000
15 from an Australian promoter to defend the title against the Empire champion, French-born Johnny Famechon.

Draw

Famechon, a resident of Australia, drew over ten rounds with René Roque, the French lightweight champion, in
20 Paris on Monday night.

Last year Roque was outpointed by our new lightweight champion, Ken Buchanan, and this year had lost two of his three previous fights.

Asked if he was worried at the possibility of the World
25 Boxing Council – with whom our own Board of Control has a working agreement – stripping Winstone of his title for not defending it against Legra within the stipulated ninety days, Thomas said: 'Naturally we are a bit "edgy", but not too worried.'

30 ### Unrealistic

'We had to agree to the ninety days when we got the match, but they should realize that it is up to us to get the best offer we can. But Legra will be next.'

However, Thomas is still talking in terms of £30,000 for
Winstone, which I regard as completely unrealistic.   35
I hope that he and Board secretary Teddy Waltham
manage to come to some agreement.
Talking of Empire fighters, Lionel Rose, the Australian
Aborigine who recently won the world bantamweight fight
by outpointing Fighting Harada in Tokyo, has to go back   40
to the Japanese capital to make his first defence there on
2 July against a so-far unnamed challenger.
They'll soon be calling him Tokyo Rose!

Peter Wilson in the *Daily Mirror*, 12 March 1968

25 *Board of Control:* the British Board of Boxing Control. The official
organization which controls boxing titles and rules of boxing conduct in
Britain.
28 *edgy:* tense, having your nerves on edge.
43 *Tokyo Rose:* an English-speaking woman announcer who broadcast propaganda for the Japanese during the Second World War.

6

At the end of August the Master sent for me. He had a   1
special message he wanted to give me, and he told me, almost
as soon as I arrived, that I was to remind him of it if he
rambled. He wanted to give me the message before I went.
His face was now an old man's. The flesh was dried and   5
had a waxy sheen. His eyes were sunken. Yet his voice was
a good imitation of its old self, and with his heightened
insight, he knew the tone which would distress me least.
And he spoke, with his old sarcastic humour, of his reasons
for changing the position of his bed. It stood by the win- 10
dow now.
'I prefer to lie here,' said the Master, 'because I got
tired of the remarkable decoration' – he meant the painted
college arms – 'which we owe to the misguided enthusiasm
of one of my predecessors who had somewhat grandilo-   15
quent tastes. And between you and me, I also like to look
out of the window and see our colleagues walking about
in twos and threes.' He smiled without sadness and with
an extraordinary detachment. 'It makes me wonder how

20 they are grouping themselves about the coming vacancy.'

I looked into the emaciated, wasted, peaceful face. 'It is surprisingly easy to face that kind of fact,' he said. 'It seems quite natural. I assure you. So you can tell me the truth. How much has been done about choosing my 25 successor? I have only heard that Jago might be in the running – which, between ourselves, I could have guessed for myself. Will he get it?

'Either he or Crawford.'

'Crawford. Scientists are too bumptious.' It was strange 30 to hear him, even when so many of the vanities of self had gone, clinging to the prejudice of a lifetime.

I described the present position of the parties. It kept his attention and amused him. As I spoke, I did not feel anything macabre about his interest; it was more as though 35 an observer from another world was watching the human comedy.

'I hope you get Jago in,' he said. 'He'll never become wise of course. He'll always be a bit of an ass. Forget that and get him in.'

40 Then he asked:

'I expect there's a good deal of feeling?'

'Yes,' I said.

'It's remarkable. People always believe that, if only they support the successful candidate, they've got his backing 45 for ever. It's an illusion, Eliot, it's an illusion. I assure you, one feels a certain faint irritation at the faces of one's loyal supporters. They catch one's eye and smirk.'

C. P. Snow: *The Masters* (Macmillan, 1951; Penguin Books, 1956)

1 *the Master:* title given to the head of most colleges in the University of Cambridge.

25 *in the running:* have some chance of winning.

7

1 I had never been in the public ward of a hospital before, and it was my first experience of doctors who handle you without speaking to you or, in a human sense, taking any notice of

you. They only put on six glasses in my case, but after doing so they scarified the blisters and applied the glasses again. Each glass now drew out about a dessertspoonful of dark-coloured blood. As I lay down again, humiliated, disgusted and frightened by the thing that had been done to me, I reflected that now at least they would leave me alone. But no, not a bit of it. There was another treatment coming, the mustard poultice, seemingly a matter of routine like the hot bath. Two slatternly nurses had already got the poultice ready, and they lashed it round my chest as tight as a strait-jacket while some men who were wandering about the ward in shirt and trousers began to collect round my bed with half-sympathetic grins. I learned later that watching a patient having a mustard poultice was a favourite pastime in the ward. These things are normally applied for a quarter of an hour and certainly they are funny enough if you don't happen to be the person inside. For the first five minutes the pain is severe, but you believe you can bear it. During the second five minutes this belief evaporates, but the poultice is buckled at the back and you can't get it off. This is the period the onlookers enjoy most. During the last five minutes I noted a sort of numbness supervenes. After the poultice had been removed a waterproof pillow packed with ice was thrust beneath my head and I was left alone. I did not sleep, and to the best of my knowledge this was the only night of my life – I mean the only night spent in bed – in which I have not slept at all, not even a minute.

During my first hour in the hospital, I had had a whole series of different and contradictory treatments, but this was misleading, for in general you got very little treatment at all, either good or bad, unless you were ill in some interesting and instructive way. At five in the morning the nurses came round, woke the patients and took their temperatures, but did not wash them. If you were well enough you washed yourself, otherwise you depended on the kindness of some walking patient. It was generally patients, too, who carried the bedbottles and the grim bedpan, nicknamed la casserole. At eight breakfast arrived, called, army-fashion, la soupe. It was soup too, a thin vegetable soup with slimy hunks of bread floating about in it.

George Orwell: 'How the Poor Die', from *Shooting an Elephant* (Secker & Warburg, 1950)

8

Turning Point
A Degree, a Liking for People and a Talent for Organization Could Get You a Good Job with the Post Office

1   The Post Office, soon to become a public corporation, needs talented graduates or potential graduates (arts and science) with the ability and energy to carry out on-the-spot inquiries and inspection on all aspects of the organization of
5   postal and counter services, mechanizing mail, handling, training and promotion of staff. This is the work of our *Assistant Postal Controllers*. They are very much out-and-about men with a deep interest in people and processes, and a talent for organization.
10   It is a vital link job that can earn you quick promotion to high managerial posts. You should be earning over £2000 a year at thirty, with your sights on posts that carry salaries of more than double that amount. It's a challenge and we need champions to take it up. Age limits are twenty to thirty-
15 two, applicants should have a degree or be taking a degree course.

Advertisement in National Press General Post Office, 1968

9

United Sweep to their Title
West Ham 1   Manchester United 6

1   A monumental performance by Manchester United confirmed them in their Championship, virtually obliterated West Ham, and left London with the marvellous concluding statement from Matt Busby's team that if the capital is to
5 have the Cup Final then Manchester is once again the centre of the universe.

For the ragged, ragamuffin red-and-white battalions which invaded the field at the end, screaming for Busby, there has never been any doubt about that.

United had clearly spurned the thought of scrambling the solitary point they needed. They devastated West Ham with the intent, with the power, the pace, the professionalism of their play from the beginning.

A Charlton goal in the second minute, then three in ten minutes, left West Ham demoralized, concussed, and, at the heart of a ravishing first-half performance, stood Bobby Charlton. His goal was astonishing in its speed, its audacity, and the lightning reaction which Charlton displayed on seizing at a quarter-chance.

Law cut Stiles through perfectly. Stiles was blocked, the ball broke loose but offered only the tightest of chances. Charlton went at it with a feverish venom that seemed almost out of character, thrashing the ball irrevocably past Mackleworth for a quite sensational goal.

Bobby Charlton, probably the best-loved player in our game, went on to play a first half that surpassed even his performance against Portugal in the World Cup semi-final. His touch on the ball, delicate and stunning, his control (once he turned past seven successive West Ham players with the same move, that quick flick with the outside of his left foot), his command of the entire mid-field when he chose – here was a vintage performance from a most wonderfully gifted player at the very height of his maturity.

Bob Ferrier in the *Observer*, 7 May 1967

5 *Cup Final:* the final match in the Football Association competition held every year in England.

7 *red-and-white:* a reference to the colours of Manchester United football team. Scarves and rosettes in these colours are worn by club supporters.

10 *scrambling:* a term used in football to mean making just enough effort, but no more.

10 *the solitary point they needed:* the competition is based on a total score of points.

19 *quarter-chance:* a term used in certain games to mean a very small chance of scoring a goal. A more usual expression is 'half-chance'.

10

**Bathing Beauty Discovered in
Interior Decorator's Bathroom!**

1 But then the interior decorator is her husband. (Seekers
after salacious gossip can stop reading now.) As you can see,
he's a man who likes to be surrounded by beautiful things.
She likes to be surrounded by beauty too. That's why she
5 spends so much time bathing (beautifully) in their beautiful
ceramic tiled bathroom.

But he hasn't used British Ceramic Tiles because of their
looks alone. Ceramic tiles are stain-proof, steam-proof, they
are extremely easy to clean and extremely difficult to dam-
10 age. And ceramic-tiled bathrooms – or kitchens – increase
the value of a building (look at any Properties for Sale
column!).

Now *you* can put in ceramic tiles and pay for them over a
period of time, under a convenient credit purchase scheme.
15 Send for our free colour brochure – and soon you'll be
bathing beautifully too.

Advertisement in National Press, 1968

11

Attack on the Ad-Man

This trumpeter of nothingness, employed
To keep our reason dull and null and void,
This man of wind and froth and flux will sell
The wares of any who reward him well.
5 Praising whatever he is paid to praise
He hunts for ever-newer, smarter ways
To make the gilt seem gold; the shoddy, silk;
To cheat us legally; to bluff and bilk
By methods which no jury can prevent
10 Because the law's not broken, only bent.
This mind for hire, this mental prostitute
Can tell the half-lie hardest to refute;
Knows how to hide an inconvenient fact
And when to leave a doubtful claim unbacked;

Manipulates the truth but not too much,   15
And, if his patter needs the Human Touch,
Skilfully artless, artfully naïve,
Wears his convenient heart upon his sleeve,
He uses words that once were strong and fine,
Primal as sun and moon and bread and wine,   20
True, honourable, honoured, clear and clean,
And leaves them shabby, worn, diminished, mean.
He takes ideas and trains them to engage
In the long little wars big combines wage.
He keeps his logic loose, his feelings flimsy;   25
Turns eloquence to cant and wit to whimsy;
Trims language till it fits his client's pattern
And style's a glossy tart or limping slattern.
He studies our defences, finds the cracks
And where the wall is weak or worn, attacks.   30
He finds the fear that's deep, the wound that's tender,
And mastered, outmanoeuvred, we surrender.
We who have tried to choose accept his choice
And tired succumb to his untiring voice.
The dripping tap makes even granite soften.   35
We trust the brand-name we have heard so often
And join the queue of sheep that flock to buy;
We fools who know our folly, you and I.

A. S. J. Tessimond: from *Voices in a Giant City*
(Heinemann, 1947)

12

Augusto's voice from the wheelhouse sounded above the   1
beat of the sea. We were nearing the coast.

'I'll come up,' said Tomas. As he said it there was a
thump like a heavy hammer being swung against the hull.
'A piece of flotsam,' said Tomas. Augusto had brought the   5
throttles back to half-speed. Again there was a thump and a
third immediately after. Augusto coughed and then fell
down the ladder into the cabin. I caught him. Augusto was
limp as he slid to the floor. The front of my suit was soaked
in blood. Augusto's blood.   10

Tomas and I stood motionless as we processed the possibilities through our brains. I was thinking of nautical mishaps, but Tomas had a more practical bent. He knew the person concerned.

15 'It's Harry Kondit,' he said. The boat purred gently towards the shore.

'Where?' I said.

'Firing his target rifle from the cliff-top,' said Tomas. There were two more thumps and now, listening for it, I

20 heard the gun crack a long way away. The floor was slippery with blood.

Tomas was as calm as a Camembert. He said, 'If we go up to the wheelhouse we get shot. If we stay here the boat heaves itself on to the cliff at Tristos and we drown.' The

25 boat lurched against the swell.

'Can we get to the rudder control without going across the deck?'

'Too slow, in this sort of sea we have to do something quick.'

30 Without Augusto at the helm the boat was slopping and slipping beam-on to the sea. It was a plywood boat. I imagined it hitting the rocks and changing to firewood at one swipe. Augusto had stuffed a signal flag into his mouth. He bit on it hard instead of screaming through his punctured

35 lung.

Tomas was carrying the little refrigerator across the cabin, and up the four steps. How he lifted it I have no idea. It thumped into the wheelhouse and then Tomas climbed to the bridge, using it as a shield. He pushed it forward and I

40 heard a great echoing clang as one of Harry Kondit's bullets glanced off the metal. Tomas was lying full-length on the deck by now with the lowest part of the control wheel in his hand. He pulled it and the boat began to answer. Through the porthole I could see the rocks. They were very close,

45 and after each great wave the water ran off the jagged fangs like a drooling monster awaiting its prey.

Len Deighton: *Horse Under Water* (Cape, 1963; Penguin Books, 1965)

31 *beam-on:* a sailor's term meaning that a ship or boat is being driven from behind by the current.

13

Mod Verse at Five Bob

Bent on making modern poetry 'something perfectly normal to read', a new publishing house has just opened in London. It is serving out the verse in neat paperbacks at five bob a time. Well aware that under ordinary conditions a poetry book rarely sells one thousand copies, the new firm has done a print of five thousand for each of its first three books.

For the present you can't get Allison and Busby on the telephone before 7 p.m. This is because its two young directors work by day for other and much older publishers.

Mr Clive Allison is twenty-two and left Oxford two years ago. His partner is Miss Margaret Busby, also twenty-two, a Ghanaian who went to Bedford College, London.

Mr Allison isn't a newcomer to the poetry trade. While still at Oxford he ran an outfit called Harlequin Poets and was 'staggered by its success'. He believes people should read poetry – 'a quick thing in a time-conscious age' – just as they read novels and hopes to bring this about by under-cutting current luxury prices.

Actually there is already in these islands a vast interest in poetry, notably among students and other young people. It is fostered by poets who, content with very little, try to live by their art, hitch-hiking about the country to give poetry readings.

Just now fifteen of these modern troubadors are trying to form a kind of trade union called 'Poetry in Motion'. Its aim is to get a fixed rate for the job, but nobody could call them acquisitive. They want £3 plus expenses for a reading in the poet's home town and £5 plus expenses if he has to travel.

We get this from Miss Libby Houston, one of those first three poets to be published by Allison and Busby. She is def-ined as an 'underground' poet, but if Miss Houston and her verses are anything to go by this implies nothing subversive.

'It means you have no strings to pull to get you on the Third Programme,' she says. 'It implies a poet of whom the Establishment hasn't heard, even though he has a vast following in all sorts of cities in Britain.'

Miss Houston, who read English at Oxford and is twenty-five, has settled down rather. She is married to a commercial
40 artist – he did the murals at London's Flamingo Club – and shares with him a two-room flat in Holloway. By day she works as a filing clerk for the Islington Borough Council.

She was born 'at the north end of the Piccadilly Line' though she is Lowland Scots on both sides and has a re-
45 puted family link with the great Sam Houston of Texas. She has an unpublished work entitled 'Libby Houston's Book of Poems' written when she was six.

Her father was killed in the last war as a bomber pilot and the first poem in the new book is about this – 'And still I
50 don't know/where my father/flying home/took a wrong turning.'

'Briefing' in the *Observer*, 7 May 1967

Title *mod:* shortened form of 'modern', smart, fashionable (slang).

5 *a print:* print-run, the number of copies of a book printed for each impression or edition.

14 *outfit:* a group of people or an organization, such as a service unit in the Army or a business unit (US slang).

26 *fixed rate for the job:* an expression used especially among trade unionists, meaning a fair wage for a particular kind of work.

32 *'underground' poet:* a poet who does not want recognition through an established publisher; his or her work is often printed on small, privately owned presses. The term 'underground' is often used to mean subversive.

35 *the Third Programme:* a BBC radio service now called Radio 3 which broadcasts music, drama, talks, etc., often of specialized interest.

36 *the Establishment:* in politics, the people who, though they often do not hold high government posts, influence the decisions made in government; in the arts, the people who are recognized as the most influential figures in their own artistic field.

43 *the Piccadilly Line:* one of the lines on London's underground transport system.

45 *Sam Houston:* one of the first people to develop the West in America; Houston, Texas, is named after him.

14

When You Make a Call

1 *First check the code (if any) and number.*

Lift the receiver and *listen for dialling tone* (a continuous purring).

Dial carefully and allow the dial to return freely.
Then wait for another tone: 5
Ringing tone (burr-burr) the number is being called.
Engaged tone (a repeated single note) try again a few
minutes later.
Number unobtainable tone (steady note) replace receiver,
re-check the code and number, and then re-dial. 10

After dialling a trunk call there will be a pause before you
hear a tone; during this time the trunk equipment will be
connecting your call.

At the end of the call, replace the receiver securely because
timing of calls stops when the caller hangs up. 15

When You Answer the Telephone
Always give your name or telephone number.

If you hear a series of rapid pips, the call is coming from a
coinbox telephone. Wait until the pips stop and then give
your name or telephone number. 20

General Post Office: *Dialling Instructions and Call Charges*
(GPO, 1970)

1 *the code:* the three letters in an English telephone number which
used to represent the name of the exchange; now replaced by an all-
figure code.

19 *coinbox telephone:* public telephones in Britain are operated by
coins, not tokens.

15

May I Help You?
Clare Shepherd Invites your Questions

Address your letters to Clare Shepherd, *Woman's Realm*, 189 1
High Holborn, London, WC1. If you would like a reply by
post, please enclose a stamped, addressed envelope. All
letters will be treated in the utmost confidence and your
identity will never be disclosed. 5

I was twenty when the man I was engaged to fell in love with
another girl. I am now twenty-nine and still unmarried for I have
never felt the same about any other man as I did about my ex-
fiancé, although I have known quite a few. I have recently started
going out with a man who works with me. We have known one 10

another a long time, and have always got on well together. He has asked me to marry him, but although I like him a great deal and enjoy his company, I am not in love with him. I long to be married and have a home and family. Do you think it is absolutely neces-
15 sary to be romantically in love with the man you marry?

If you mean is it necessary to have the heady, 'I'll die if I don't see him tomorrow' kind of love for the man you are thinking of marrying, the answer is no. Many very happy marriages are based upon companionship and the desire for
20 a home and family. In marriage there must be a real sense of pleasure in being together plus a definite physical attraction. Our reader must make her decision upon the basis of what lies between this man and herself. Does she find him physically attractive? How sad would she be if he went out
25 of her life? Does she look forward to sharing her daily life with him? Can she depend on him to be a loving husband? These are the questions she must ask herself. Comparisons with the nostalgic love for a lost young man are useless.

Please can you tell me what to do? I have been going out with
30 my boy friend for about three months and am very fond of him. I enjoy every minute of his company and feel that we get on very well. However, he has confided in me that he never has any urge to be intimate with me or any other woman, and I feel this is not normal. I would like to think he does not attempt this out of
35 respect for me, but I am worried by his attitude, for if we married I should want to lead a normal life and have a family. He is twenty-two and I am twenty-one.

Men and women vary greatly in their sexual drives and it may be simply that your boy friend is maturing late. On the
40 other hand, it is possible that there is something wrong either physically or mentally. Continue to enjoy his friendship, but unless he changes, do not contemplate marriage without medical advice. It is almost impossible for a normal young woman to be happily married to a man who has no
45 interest at all in sexual love.

Clare Shepherd in *Woman's Realm*, June 1967

16

'Mr Mulholland was a great one for his tea,' she said at length. 'Never in my life have I seen anyone drink as much tea as dear, sweet Mr Mulholland.'

'I suppose he left fairly recently,' Billy said. He was still puzzling his head about the two names. He was positive now that he had seen them in the newspapers – in the headlines.

'Left?' she said, arching her brows. 'But my dear boy, he never left. He's still here. Mr Temple is also here. They're on the third floor, both of them together.'

Billy set down his cup slowly on the table, and stared at his landlady. She smiled back at him, and then she put out one of her white hands and patted him comfortingly on the knee. 'How old are you, my dear?' she asked.

'Seventeen.'

'Seventeen!' she cried. 'Oh, it's the perfect age! Mr Mulholland was also seventeen. But I think he was a trifle shorter than you are, in fact I'm sure he was, and his teeth weren't *quite* so white. You have the most beautiful teeth, Mr Weaver, did you know that?'

'They're not as good as they look,' Billy said. 'They've got simply masses of fillings in them at the back.'

'Mr Temple, of course, was a little older,' she said, ignoring his remark. 'He was actually twenty-eight. And yet I never would have guessed it if he hadn't told me, never in my whole life. There wasn't a *blemish* on his body.'

'A what?' Billy said.

'His skin was *just* like a baby's.'

There was a pause. Billy picked up his teacup and took another sip of his tea, then he set it down again gently in its saucer. He waited for her to say something else, but she seemed to have lapsed into another of her silences. He sat there staring straight ahead of him into the far corner of the room, biting his lower lip.

'That parrot,' he said at last. 'You know something? It had me completely fooled when I first saw it through the window from the street. I could have sworn it was alive.'

'Alas, no longer.'

'It's most terribly clever the way it's been done,' he said.
40 'It doesn't look in the least bit dead. Who did it?'

'I did.'

'*You* did?'

'Of course,' she said. 'And have you met my little Basil as
well?' She nodded towards the dachshund curled up so
45 comfortably in front of the fire. Billy looked at it. And suddenly, he realized that this animal had all the time been just
as silent and motionless as the parrot. He put out a hand and
touched it gently on the top of its back. The back was hard
and cold, and when he pushed the hair to one side with his
50 fingers, he could see the skin underneath, greyish-black and
dry and perfectly preserved.

'Good gracious me,' he said. 'How absolutely fascinating.'
He turned away from the dog and stared with deep admiration at the little woman beside him on the sofa. 'It must
55 be most awfully difficult to do a thing like that.'

'Not in the least,' she said. 'I stuff *all* my little pets myself when they pass away. Will you have another cup of
tea?'

'No, thank you,' Billy said. The tea tasted faintly of bitter
60 almonds, and he didn't much care for it.

'You did sign the book, didn't you?'

'Oh, yes.'

'That's good. Because later on, if I happen to forget what
you were called, then I can always come down here and look
65 it up. I still do that almost every day with Mr Mulholland
and Mr . . . Mr . . .'

'Temple,' Billy said. 'Gregory Temple. Excuse my asking, but haven't there been *any* other guests here except
them in the last two or three years?'

70 Holding her teacup high in one hand, inclining her head
slightly to the left, she looked up at him out of the corners of
her eyes and gave him another gentle little smile.

'No, my dear,' she said. 'Only you.'

Roald Dahl: *Kiss Kiss* (Michael Joseph, 1960; Penguin
Books, 1962)

1 *a great one for his tea:* very fond of his tea (colloquial).
59 *bitter almonds:* the characteristic taste of cyanide, a deadly poison.

17

Illegitimacy

Girl, 19 (father unknown, grew up with sister and two half- 1
brothers)

I want to know who my father is, what he looks like, and
why he did not want me. As a child I missed having relations about me. I know now they did not want anything to 5
do with us after my birth and treated us like black sheep,
though they knew we were in desperate need of support.
Being illegitimate has not affected me career-wise; ironically
it has helped me; it has made me more tolerant towards
other people's difficulties. But the word 'bastard' is con- 10
tinually used in films and books to describe undesirable
people, and it does hurt.

Woman, 22 (father unknown, mother married another man
two months before child was born)

Horrid, deep, dirty feelings of guilt. Guilt at being a mishap, 15
mistake, unwanted inconvenience. Anger with my mother
for allowing this to happen to her. Anger with my father for
indulging himself and then not even wanting to see me.
There's this indescribable feeling of being only a half a
person; one has this part of a father in one, stagnating and 20
useless. Are any other men to be trusted? Are women just a
convenience, as my mother was? Sex becomes seemingly a
wholly destructive element.

Man, 30 (father died soon after child was born, adopted by
father's relatives) 25

I learnt I was illegitimate just before I was sixteen. About a
year later I had a colossal nervous breakdown which altered
me completely. Hitherto I had had energy enough to run
about and be happy. Now life was one long battle against
weariness and depression. 30

I remember one fearful outburst I had myself, raging and
storming against my illegitimacy and my relations who had
adopted me. I accused them of making a great show of con-

ventional vainglory and yet failing to tell me satisfactorily of
35 my parents and my mother in particular. I have never really
been the same since. I am a bad mixer, shy and solitary.
When things go wrong I get bitter and feel wild and frustrated.

I am sure people who are illegitimate should be told about
40 it nicely, straightly and soon. This is much better than the
shock of coming on it unawares. People should do everything to avoid illegitimates feeling different. It is sad to say
but I think things have been made awkward by the high
standards of the Christian religion which is in other ways so
45 splendid.

Marjorie P. Schofield: extracts from material for a book on
illegitimacy, published in the *Observer*, 9 April 1967

1 *half-brothers:* brothers by one parent only.
6 *black sheep:* in general, a person of bad character; in particular, as
here, a person of whom their family is ashamed.

18

1 With the recent revival of the 'Batman' saga at a London
cinema, it seems a good moment to talk about that mysterious
subject, Pop Culture. *Life International* had a brave shot
recently at a definition. Pop Culture, it declared, is 'an
5 umbrella term covering nearly anything which is currently
in style'. Surely one can do a little better than that? The
entire phenomenon of Pop Culture has begun to loom so
large in our appreciation of the visual arts that I'd like to
devote a little time to exploring the subject.
10 What, for instance, are the things which divide Pop
Culture from Mass Culture, or even from culture in general?
Pop, we must admit, is a word which now carries with it
certain special connotations – the revolt of the young against
the old, for example, and the fact that the age-gap is now
15 beginning to count for more than the class-gap. Mass
Culture makes itself available to everyone, Pop Culture does
no such thing – it has a fierce clannishness which is not the
least of its fascinations. In fact, one of the most interesting
things about Pop is that it is basically anti-art. One might

even argue that the real reason why it fascinates artists is that they have now become anti-art also.

Pop, for example, is hostile to the idea of permanence. Art is, among other things, a form of human activity which protests at the cruel destructiveness of time. Shakespeare tells the young hero of the Sonnets:

So long as men can breathe, or eyes can see,
So long lives this, and this gives life to thee.

Such things as advertisements, posters, pop songs, Carnaby Street clothes (all of them part of the Pop ethos) invite us to an avid enjoyment by parading the fact that their creators don't expect them to last. And this, in turn, relates to the kind of society we live in. This is the first age, I think, which has erected the enjoyment of the moment into a moral imperative (or at least the first age in which the imperative has been so devoutly obeyed).

It is interesting to examine Pop Culture to see what it borrows and what it invents. The involvement of 'high culture' with Pop in the postwar era is a thing which has been much discussed. What has been less thoroughly examined is the tendency of Pop to take what it needed from the avant-garde. Ever since the beginnings of modernism, avant-garde ideas have been infiltrating the commercial sphere. The typography of the Dadaists was not slow to make its impact on the glossy magazines of the twenties. In the same way, the shapes and colours used by Delaunay soon began to turn up in the fabric designs of the 'jazz age'. Surrealism had a tremendous impact on the shop windows of New York, London and Paris, and of course the influence of the movement is clearly to be seen in the clothes designed by Schiaparelli.

Edward Lucie-Smith in *The Times*, 15 February 1966

1 '*Batman*': an American television and comic-strip hero.

3 *Pop Culture*: a current trend among young people towards colourful, new and unconventional fashions, many of which are short-lived. 'Pop' ideas range from a skirt using the design of the British flag to paintings based on comic-strips.

28 *Carnaby Street*: a shopping street in London's West End, which started off specializing in cheap, colourful and unusual clothes, but since

it became a great tourist attraction, now sells everything from Indian scarves to plastic reproductions of London street-signs.

29 *ethos:* the atmosphere or feeling of a society or group.

41 *avant-garde:* a term applied to experimental work in literature, theatre, cinema, art, etc. It is nearly always too far ahead of its time to be appreciated by the general public.

43 *Dadaists:* ('dada' – figurative meaning, 'fad', *French*) an extremist anti-art movement which started in 1915. Its members set out to outrage people with ideas such as a reproduction of the *Mona Lisa* decorated with a moustache, and an exhibition where a chopper was provided for the spectators to smash the exhibits with.

45 *Delaunay:* (Robert) a French artist (1885–1941) who was responsible for the type of Cubism known as Orphism, which considered colour more important than form.

46 *'jazz age':* a term often used for the 1920s when jazz became widely popular.

50 *Schiaparelli:* a famous French dress designer.

19

1 She looked at the rows of new books. 'Have you anything really shocking, Reggie? I adore mucky books, and you never have any in stock.'

She was wearing a scent like burnt roses; it seemed to fill
5 the room, overlaying the smell of books and Pollywog paste.

'Do you know any good ones, Joe?' she asked me.

'I like my pornography in real life,' I said.

'Well, what are we waiting for?'

Reggie was watching us with a curious intentness; the
10 Library was the clearing-house for all the town's gossip. I decided to change the subject.

'Did you know I'm playing Joshua?' I flexed my biceps and threw out my chest. 'The strength of a giant and the heart of a child. Led astray by a wicked woman –'

15 'Damn the Casting Committee,' she said, '*I* wanted to lead you astray. Why didn't they give me the part?'

'The Housekeeper's much nicer,' Reggie said. 'Needs real acting. Anyone can play Leda.'

'Maybe,' Eva said gloomily, 'but I'm fed up with being
20 wholesome. I *long* to be seductive and tempting. What's Alice got that I haven't got?'

'Who's Alice?' I asked.

'You've met her, you dope. Tall and slim and blonde.

32

Used to act in Rep. You might have noticed her if you hadn't been making eyes at Susan.' 25

'Is she married?'

'I hope so, she's been living with him nearly ten years. George Aisgill; you've met him too, he came to the last Social Evening. Lots of money. They seem happy enough –' She stopped, as if she were on the verge of indiscretion. 30

'I remember her now,' I said. 'She seemed a bit offhand. In fact, definitely cold.'

'You mean that she didn't succumb immediately to your charms,' Reggie said. His tone was light. I couldn't take offence but I resolved to be more careful in front of him in 35 future.

'You should never look at one woman when you're talking to another,' Eva said. 'No wonder the poor darling was offhand. Alice is a very sweet person indeed and I won't hear a word against her, so there.' 40

'She's a damned good actress,' Reggie said. 'God, she was wonderful in *The Playground*. Absolutely *exuded* sex. Two old dears walked out in the middle of Act Two.'

John Braine: *Room at the Top* (Eyre & Spottiswoode, 1957; Penguin Books, 1959)

23 *dope*: fool (slang).
24 *Rep.*: (shortened form of repertory) a provincial theatre company which puts on different plays, each for a short time.

20

Cliff: The Star with no Escape

Cliff Richard clenched his fists with all the determination he 1 could muster and said: 'I must get out of show business as soon as possible. But how do I do it?'

Richard, twenty-six, who plans retirement after nine years as a pop music idol, wants to teach religion. Success, however, 5 is having its problems.

'Right now I am making a film for Billy Graham. It's not a documentary, but a real story. But what do I do if it is so successful they want me to make another one?'

There's another complication. Although Cliff intends a 10

clean break, he is committed by a long-term contract to go on making records.

'If the records don't sell, I will be happy to tear up the contract, but if I am still popular I will not be able to give up being a pop star of sorts.'

Attitudes

In his manager's elegantly furnished office in London's Savile Row, Cliff talked for the first time of why he wants to give up the glitter of stardom.

'Five years ago, I was sitting in a stuffy hotel room in Melbourne, Australia. I wondered aloud if I could get in touch with my father, who had died a few months earlier. One of the Shadows at that time, Brian "Liquorice" Locking, told me it would be wrong.

'He pulled out a Bible and showed me about five places where they warned against trying to contact the dead. Man, that impressed me.

'Here was an old book with an answer to a modern problem. I started reading the Bible and it began to change my attitudes.'

Two years ago, Richard says, he became a 'true Christian'. Now he feels that he must give up £100,000 a year in show business for a three-year college course which will qualify him as a £16-a-week teacher.

Interests

No more crowd-pulling tours. No more fan riots. And no more TV spectaculars like the one in which he starred this week.

He gets angry at being called 'Vicar Richard' and 'The High Priest of Pop'.

'Do you know a lot of people think this is a big gimmick. That I'm not sincere about it. Well I am.'

In the Billy Graham film, Richard plays a double-crossing, drug-peddling, bed-hopping materialist. He doesn't actually get converted in the end, but, says Cliff, there is a clear glimmer of hope.

When Richard retires he says he intends to keep his possessions.

'I have lots of business interests, property and investments. No, I shan't sell. What would I do with the money? You don't have to be poor to be a Christian.'

A pause, then: 'Honestly, we have never worked for money as a prime consideration. If we had, the Shadows and I would be millionaires by now.

'But I don't think I would be a happy millionaire if I had not become a Christian.'

Michael Hellicar in the *Daily Mirror*, 27 May 1967

5 *pop music:* usually electronically amplified music with a strong rhythm, much influenced by American Negro music; in general, any music which young people like to listen or dance to.

7 *Billy Graham:* an internationally known American preacher.

18 *Savile Row:* a street in London's West End famous for its expensive tailors' shops.

23 *the Shadows:* the group who used to provide the musical backing to Cliff Richard's songs.

36 *fan riots:* demonstrations by enthusiastic admirers, often for a popular singer.

37 *TV:* abbreviation of television.

43 *double-crossing:* cheating or betraying, usually by pretending to be on someone's side while secretly working against them.

21

The process of indoctrination began immediately after capture when, to their surprise, the Chinese would greet each prisoner with a smile, a cigarette and a handshake. There were good grounds for this surprise since the North Koreans they had met earlier, having little food or amenities, often shot their prisoners in cold blood. After shaking hands, the captors would congratulate their captives on having escaped from capitalist bondage and kept repeating to them such simple slogans as 'Be a fighter for peace.' Anyone who showed hesitation was asked: 'Are you for peace? Of course you are. Every intelligent person is. Then, naturally you will fight for peace. Good! You are henceforth a true fighter in the cause of peace. Now you will have an opportunity to display the courage of your convictions and fight for peace!' The prisoner was then asked

to sign a peace appeal, and if he resisted he would be told that by signing he would simply be reaffirming a universal desire of all thinking human beings. To many this seemed a plausible request and it was explained that the Com-
20 munists wanted him to sign one such appeal only. These requests were so innocuous in appearance that many signed if only to escape the constant badgering, but they soon found that, having put their heads in the noose, it was difficult to escape. During this initial friendly period the
25 Chinese tried to find out everything possible about the captives, but they were less concerned about military facts than those which revealed something about the individual's home background, thus giving them something to work on when indoctrination proper began. The prisoner was
30 ordered to fill in a detailed questionnaire on a sheet of paper with a false heading of the International Red Cross, being told that the information was needed so that the Chinese Red Cross could inform his next of kin. The questions dealt with such matters as his father's occupation,
35 the family's annual income and his own educational background, so that some idea of the prisoner's socio-economic status could be obtained. Later, other and more detailed questionnaires were issued, and the prisoners were asked to write autobiographies; some wrote three or even more.
40 The actual process of indoctrination was apparently based on the more severe technique used by the Russians on their prisoners during the Second World War, when they had tried to bring about subversion by the formation of the 'German Liberation Committee'. Chinese interrogators
45 had often been educated in the United States and all had a thorough knowledge of American affairs down to the smallest details of regional customs.

J. A. C. Brown: *Techniques of Persuasion* (Penguin Books, 1963)

22

MPs Squabble over War Toys

All the child psychologists in the House of Commons had
the time of their lives today during a private members'
debate calling for a ban on war toys. Mrs Anne Kerr, mover
of the motion, was not pulling her punches. She jolted the
house on to its toes by telling members that this might be
the last time they would be able to discuss the question of
violence before the Third World War broke out.

This was pretty rough stuff, said Mr Quintin Hogg, who
declared that he did not feel much safer after the honourable
lady had put her proposals for survival. After this splendid
start she had produced 'an extraordinarily small brown
mouse'.

The word 'ban' was the excuse, Mr Hogg said, for much
of the woolliest thinking that went on in the Commons, and
he continued on a course that came pretty close to demanding
a ban on Mrs Kerr.

This motion reflected a very common frame of mind, the
member for St Marylebone said. Because we could not
control adults or perhaps ourselves, the reaction was to
take it out on the children. He was not going to become an
apostle of the permissive society but he felt that the Third
World War was not going to be stopped by a ban on toy
soldiers and imitation tommy-guns.

Mrs Kerr denounced the Government for not producing
the Minister for Disarmament to answer her case. In the
event, she had to put up with Mr Darling from the Board of
Trade, who gave her a very dusty answer and spoke of the
'sensitive social conscience' of the British toy industry.

Taking a leaf out of the Duke's book, Mr Darling told
Mrs Kerr that you could not go around banning toy
imports for moral or social reasons. Why, somebody might
do the same to us.

Mrs Kerr told how her mother had been out shopping
for her. She had brought back flame-throwers, bombs and
booby-traps. The Kerr homestead was full of these horrifying things. Her hairdresser and the Jehovah's Witnesses
were all sure the world was coming to an end.

She took neither of these very seriously – the Commons
sighed with relief at this – but there seemed to be a general
40 feeling that we were not long for this world. Her hairdresser's boy friend had failed to keep a date and then on
one occasion when he did turn up, he stole her money. It
was apparently all to do with war toys and in particular the
orgy of them we had every Christmas.

45 Mr John Tilney, from the Conservative benches, tried
to console her. Mankind was naturally pugnacious, he said.
Just look what happened at church fêtes; civilized people
paying sixpence to break crockery.

Mr Cranley Onslow was very stern with Mrs Kerr; a
50 muddled and misconceived motion, he said. You might
as well outlaw golliwogs, cowboys and Indians, Grimm's
Fairy Tales or cops and robbers.

Hugh Noyes in *The Times*, 4 July 1967

Title *MPs:* abbreviation for Members of Parliament.
3 *mover of the motion:* a person who puts forward a proposal to be discussed and voted on at a meeting.
4 *not pulling her punches:* attacking forcefully.
9 *honourable:* traditional way of addressing a Member of Parliament
during Parliamentary sittings.
26 *Board of Trade:* government department in Britain mainly concerned with trade.
27 *dusty answer:* reproving (slang).
29 *the Duke:* the Duke of Edinburgh.
34 *flame-throwers:* weapons which throw a stream of burning kerosene.
36 *Jehovah's Witnesses:* a religious sect.
45 *Conservative:* one of the two major political parties in Britain.
51 *Grimm's Fairy Tales:* a famous collection of children's stories
compiled by the Grimm brothers.

23

Ban War Toys, says Mrs Kerr

1 Labour MP Mrs Anne Kerr (Rochester and Chatham)
called for a ban on the sale, manufacture, import, export
and advertisement of what she called 'war' toys in the
Commons yesterday.

5 Moving a resolution to this effect, she said, 'My mother
has gone round toy shops and has bought me an armoury

of modern war toys which I think are absolutely horrifying.'

Every Christmas she said, was a 'war-toy orgy'. We should not try to impress upon children our own acceptance of violence.   10

Export Market

Mr George Darling, Minister of State, Board of Trade, said that last year £16 million worth of British toys were exported overseas. The UK toy industry produced some war toys, both for the home and export markets.   15

'To ban imports for strictly moral or social reasons, which would have to be proved, might well invite retaliatory action against our own exports,' he said.

Morning Star, 4 July 1967

1 *Labour:* one of the two major political parties in Britain.
1 *MP:* abbreviation for Member of Parliament.
14 *UK:* abbreviation for United Kingdom.

24

Penalty Area

'There is nothing, absolutely nothing, which will burn a   1
voter quite so much as the suggestion that a political leader, by virtue of money or power, is getting by with something that would find the average man facing harsh penalties.' Thus wrote the astute Jerry Greene of the Washington   5
bureau of the *New York Daily News* twenty-four hours before the Kennedy kitchen cabinet, sweating out its public-relations strategy in the family compound on Cape Cod, came reluctantly to the same conclusion.

Since the first word of this accident was printed, this had   10
always been the main threat to Senator Kennedy's political survival. A popular suspicion of guilt is always aggravated by the silence of the party of the first part. This is an axiom among everybody from errant husbands to small boys home late from school. Why should its obvious sense be so   15
mysteriously withheld from the great manipulators of power?

It can only be, as the melancholy history of the Johnson

administration will show – in every blunder from the
Jenkins case to the Fortas resignation – that the immediate
instinct of the fixer is to fix even the unfixable. Men who
trust not to their judgements but to the ministrations of
public-relations experts come to acquire a reflex which
says: 'Relax, wait a while and become a beneficiary of the
lapse of time.' Andrew Mellon thought it would happen,
so did Edward VIII, so did Ike's Sherman Adams, so did
LBJ and Abe Fortas, and so did Edward Kennedy.

To work his way out of this maze of sophistication to a
glimpse of the obvious, it took Edward Kennedy six days,
a family conference, the placing of innumerable telephone
calls, warnings of the Democratic leaders in Congress,
summoning of former Assistant Attorney-General Burke
Marshall, three family lawyers, and finally the old Secretary
of Defence, Robert McNamara. At last, it was decided, the
shrewdest technique was no technique at all, but a simple
response to the first promptings of conscience.

So he made a clean breast, and the leaders of the Democratic Party breathed again. Perhaps they hope that Time
– which worked so quickly and cruelly against them – will
now stretch himself and purify the penitent Senator and
make him clean and worthy by 1972. There is no expertise
in these matters. Three and a half years is a long time to
harbour and nourish a grudge. The Republicans, for their
part, are being impeccably high-minded in public. In
private, they lean back into the comfortable reminder that a
Republican, like the elephant which is his symbol, never
forgets.

'Alistair Cooke's America' in the *Guardian*, 28 July 1969

7 *cabinet:* a group of ministers chosen by the head of a government to
be responsible for policy decisions. Here, *kitchen cabinet* means a family
council.

8 *Cape Cod:* a holiday resort on the north-east coast of the United
States.

10 *this accident:* Edward Kennedy, the youngest brother of the late
American President, John F. Kennedy, was involved in a car accident in
July 1969 which resulted in the death of one of the former secretaries of
his brother, Robert Kennedy.

18 *the Johnson administration:* the administration of President Lyndon
B. Johnson which ended in 1968.

19 *the Jenkins case . . . the Fortas resignation:* political scandals which took place during the Johnson administration.

25 *Andrew Mellon:* an American multi-millionaire who was Secretary to the Treasury at the time of a notorious scandal known as the 'Teapot Dome' case.

26 *Edward VIII:* King of England, who abdicated in 1936 in order to marry an American divorcee.

26 *Ike:* the nickname of Dwight D. Eisenhower, President of the United States from 1952 to 1960.

26 *Sherman Adams:* the central figure in a political scandal under the Eisenhower administration.

27 *L B J:* the initials of Lyndon B. Johnson; also his nickname.

31 *Democratic leaders:* the leaders of the Democratic Party, one of the two major parties in American politics.

37 *made a clean breast:* confessed everything.

43 *Republicans:* the other major American political party.

25

Spiced Spare-Ribs

1. Wipe the ribs and place skin side up in a roasting tin. Sprinkle with salt and cook at 400°F (Mark 6) for 30 mins.

2. Gently fry the onion in lard until soft but not coloured.

3. Blend together all other ingredients except the prunes and apricots.

Add to onions, simmer a few minutes.

4. Pour off excess fat from ribs, cut ribs into portions. Leave in tin and pour sauce over. Continue to cook at 400°F (Mark 6) for 30 mins.

5. Add drained fruit, spoon sauce over and cook for a further 30 mins. Serve with parsleyed new potatoes.

N.B. To really enjoy spare-ribs, nibble every scrap off the bone. *Use your hands.*

Serves 4

3 lb spare-ribs
Salt
1 large onion, peeled and sliced
1 oz lard
4 level tablespoonfuls Demerara sugar
2 level teaspoonfuls salt
1 level teaspoonful paprika
1 level tablespoonful concentrated tomato paste

41

2 tablespoonfuls Worcester sauce
½ pint of water
25 2 tablespoonfuls malt vinegar
4 tablespoonfuls lemon juice
¼ lb prunes, soaked and stoned
¼ lb dried apricots, soaked

Brandy Bombs – An Armenian Delicacy

30 1. Blanch, roast and chop almonds finely, and mix with cinammon. Cream the Spry, add 1 coffee cup icing sugar and cream thoroughly.

2. Mix in 2 egg yolks then brandy or water. Gradually add
35 the flour. (It will be easier to mix this with your hands.)

3. Add the nuts and cinammon mixture and mix thoroughly.

4. Roll into small flat shapes and bake in moderate oven 350°F (Mark 4) for about 25 mins. Whilst biscuits are still hot, coat thickly in the rest of the icing sugar.

40 5. Allow to become quite cold. Store in air-tight tins.

1 lb Self-raising flour
½ lb Spry
1 lb icing sugar
½ small coffee-cup brandy (this can be omitted and same
45   quantity cold water used)
2 egg yolks
1 teaspoon cinammon
¼ lb almonds

Vera Levine

31 *Spry:* the brand name of a cooking fat.

26

The Magic Mr Clore. . . That Was

1 The Queen will journey to Regent's Park Zoo on Monday. There she will open the Charles Clore Pavilion for Mammals. Good works clearly are no guarantee of good profits. Last week Clore's Tees-side shipyard, Furness, announced
5 losses of £6·5 million.

Charles Clore is rich. Yet he seems to have lost that magic touch. Those of his vast interests that pop into public view are looking decidedly tarnished these days. At a rough guess they have lost him something approaching £10 million over the past five years – most of it, fortunately, on paper.

Mr Leonard Sainer, solicitor, and Clore's closest adviser, wouldn't argue with the figure, although 'neither of us have ever stopped to work it out'. It looks a lot, but 'If Clore's made mistakes,' says one City man, 'it makes mere mortals like us feel less inferior.'

Sears Holdings is the hub of Clore's empire. By holding the bulk of the voting shares, worth around £5 million, he controls assets of £158 million. From the centre radiate a host of interests, including that bad-apple shipyard that cost £3·5 million to modernize and lost £6·5 million.

Other interests include Bentley Engineering, famous for hosiery knitting machinery, Shaw and Kilburn the Vauxhall distributors, jewellers Mappin and Webb and Garrard, department store Robinson and Cleaver, and in America the Consolidated Laundries Corporation. However, the biggest asset is the 69 per cent stake in the British Shoe Corporation, the company that controls at least half of Britain's shoe sales and is now the home of Clore's most recent coup, Lewis's Investment Trust, the store group that includes Selfridges.

Incredibly, Clore's master company, Sears, now seems to be approaching the position that would once have excited Clore himself as a potential takeover proposition. The return on capital employed has been dwindling steadily. In 1960 it was 25 per cent. Last year it slumped to just under 10 per cent. The man who built his life on taking sleeping assets and putting them to work is in danger of letting his own assets nod off.

Anthony Bambridge in the *Observer*, 7 May 1967

2 *Charles Clore:* an English multi-millionaire.
15 *City:* the financial centre of London.
20 *bad-apple:* something all right to look at but bad inside (idiom).
23 *Vauxhall:* the name of a British car manufacturer.

27

Sir,

I wish to refer to your last Sunday's article headed 'The magic Mr Clore ... that was'.

The tone of the article is clearly offensive and derogatory of Mr Charles Clore. You are, of course, at liberty to make any fair comment you desire, but my particular complaint is the manner in which I have been drawn into the article, which is interpolated with quotations attributed to me and gives the impression that the article is the result of a fairly long interview with me. In fact the contrary is the case.

Your Business Editor, Mr Bambridge, spoke to me on the telephone and raised with me the question of the losses of the shipyard. On the footing that he represented a responsible newspaper, I explained that we had provided this year for losses which would normally be spread over three years, in order to make provisions for all ascertainable losses in relation to existing contracts.

Mr Bambridge then suggested that Mr Clore's holding in the Sears Group had shown substantial losses, and my comment was that this applied to most investors, whose portfolios were showing a substantial percentage of loss on their peak valuations. Mr Bambridge suggested that the loss would be of the order of £10 million, but I told him I could make no comment as to the figure, especially as these were paper losses and Mr Clore's policy was not to buy in order to sell as soon as he saw a profit, but to hold for long-term investment, ignoring fluctuations of the stock market.

Mr Bambridge went on very briefly to mention other businesses, including Anglo Norness and City Centre Properties. My comment was that one could not expect to be successful in every field, but that we hoped the setbacks in these companies were only temporary.

I think I have given a fair summary of my short conversation with Mr Bambridge, and I would like you and him to know that I take the strongest objection to factual discussions on serious business topics being incorporated

out of context in the type of patronizing article which you
published last week.   40
Leonard Sainer

Letter in the *Observer*, 14 May 1967

14 *on the footing:* on the understanding (idiom).
22 *portfolios:* lists of shares held in various companies (commercial usage).
29 *stock market:* place where stocks and shares are publicly bought and sold.

28

Lieutenant Scheisskopf longed desperately to win parades   1
and sat up half the night working on it while his wife waited
amorously for him in bed thumbing through Krafft-Ebbing
to her favourite passages. He read books on marching. He
manipulated boxes of chocolate soldiers until they melted   5
in his hands and then manoeuvered in ranks of twelve a
set of plastic cowboys he had bought under an assumed
name and kept locked away from everyone's eyes during the
day. Leonardo's exercises in anatomy proved indispensable.
One evening he felt the need for a live model and directed   10
his wife to march around the room.

'Naked?' she asked hopefully.

Lieutenant Scheisskopf smacked his hands over his eyes
in exasperation. It was the despair of Lieutenant Scheisskopf's life to be chained to a woman who was incapable of   15
looking beyond her own dirty sexual desires to the titanic
struggles for the unattainable in which noble man could
become heroically engaged.

'Why don't you ever whip me?' she pouted one night.

'Because I haven't the time,' he snapped at her im-   20
patiently. 'I haven't the time. Don't you know there's a
parade going on?'

And he really did not have the time. There it was,
Sunday already, with only seven days left in the week to
get ready for the next parade. He had no idea where the   25
hours went. Finishing last in three successive parades had
given Lieutenant Scheisskopf an unsavoury reputation,

and he considered every means of improvement, even
nailing the twelve men in each rank to a long two-by-four
30 beam of seasoned oak to keep them in line. The plan was
not feasible, for making a ninety-degree turn would have
been impossible, without nickel-alloy swivels inserted in
the small of every man's back, and Lieutenant Scheisskopf
was not sanguine at all about obtaining that many nickel-
35 alloy swivels from the Quartermaster or enlisting the co-
operation of the surgeons at the hospital . . . .

Lieutenant Scheisskopf's preparations were elaborate
and clandestine. All the cadets in his squadron were sworn
to secrecy and rehearsed in the dead of night on the
40 auxiliary parade ground. They marched in darkness that
was pitch and bumped into each other blindly, but they
did not panic, and they were learning to march without
swinging their hands. Lieutenant Scheisskopf's first
thought had been to have a friend of his in the sheet-metal
45 shop sink pegs of nickel alloy into each man's thighbones
and link them to the wrists by strands of copper wire with
exactly three inches of play, but there wasn't time – there
never was enough time – and good copper wire was hard to
come by in wartime.

50 He remembered also that the men, so hampered, would
be unable to fall properly during the impressive fainting
ceremony preceding the marching and that an inability to
faint properly might affect the unit's rating as a whole.

And all week long he chortled with repressed delight at
55 the officers' club. Speculation grew rampant among his
closest friends.

'I wonder what that shithead is up to,' Lieutenant Engle
said.

Lieutenant Scheisskopf responded with a knowing smile
60 to the queries of his colleagues. 'You'll find out Sunday,'
he promised. 'You'll find out.'

Lieutenant Scheisskopf unveiled his epochal surprise
that Sunday with all the aplomb of an inexperienced
impresario. He said nothing while the other squadrons
65 ambled past the reviewing stand crookedly in their custom-
ary manner. He gave no sign even when the first ranks of
his own squadron hove into sight with their swingless

46

marching and the first stricken gasps of alarm were hissing
from his startled fellow officers. He held back even then
until the bloated colonel with the big fat moustache whirled   70
upon him savagely with a purpling face, and then he
offered the explanation that made him immortal.

'Look, Colonel,' he announced. 'No hands.'

Joseph Heller: *Catch-22* (Cape, 1962; Corgi, 1964)

3 *Krafft-Ebbing:* a German writer on sexual deviations.
9 *Leonardo:* Leonardo da Vinci, the Renaissance Italian artist.
29 *two-by-four:* two inches wide by four feet long.
57 *shithead:* an insulting term for someone (slang). Shit usually
means excrement, but is sometimes used as a slang term for marijuana.

29

Yesterday the Royal Albert Hall reached the centenary of its   1
foundation-stone laying – a ceremony performed by Queen
Victoria in the presence of ten thousand people.

Over the years the Hall has deviated from those Arts and
Sciences to which – at the Prince Consort's earnest desire –   5
it had been dedicated. Today it is the home of events as
varied as big music (notably the Proms), professional
boxing matches, selected political rallies, reunions of old
warriors and national conventions of our Townswomen's
Guilds.   10

It is easy to see why this huge domed brick cylinder –
clean and convincing in its simplicity, according to Nikolaus
Pevsner – has become known as 'London's village hall'
and has won a special place in the affections of the nation.

Aptly enough, Mr F. J. Mundy, the manager, is himself   15
a big man, lately retired from the RAF. He told us the
Hall itself was not celebrating this centenary, partly
because it has others to choose from. This one is being
left to the BBC Home Service, which today, and again on
1 June, will broadcast a fifty-five-minute programme on the   20
history of 'Albert's Great Hall'.

Mr Mundy and the private corporation which runs the
hall hope instead to celebrate the centenary in 1971, of the
actual opening.

25　　The Albert Hall has always operated, usually with success, under two major handicaps. One is the notorious echo which – as one wise manager once put it – allows some patrons 'to hear two concerts for the price of one'. The other is a seat-holding system unique in the world.

30　　At the start this was no handicap, but the means of bringing a doubtful project to fruition. People were induced to contribute to the original building fund by the offer of one seat for each £100 subscribed. With each seat went the right – which could be diminished only by Act of Parlia-

35　ment – to 'perpetual free admission'.

　　Learned counsel have held that Albert Hall seat-holders could, if they wished, unbolt their seats and take them home or if they owned a box install a bath in it. Once when a ball was to be held there, the dance floor was laid above the

40　level of the stalls. Two lady seat-holders insisted that a hole should be cut in the dance floor to give them access to their seats, and then sat there, uniquely privileged and, one imagines, supremely uncomfortable.

　　There are now about 350 of these hereditary seat-holders,

45　owning 1283 of the best seats in a total of 5606. They are free to sell their seats outright; a box with room for eight was auctioned in 1948 for £3050. They may also dispose of the tickets they don't need, through ticket agencies, though on one occasion a seat-holder was restrained by legal

50　injunction from flogging them directly to the queue outside the Hall.

Observer Review, 21 May 1967

1 *Royal Albert Hall:* a huge concert hall in London named after Prince Albert, Queen Victoria's husband. It has held a record number of 6500 people, including those standing.
5 *Prince Consort:* Prince Albert.
7 *the Proms:* the Promenade Concerts, an annual series of concerts held at the Albert Hall.
9 *Townswomen's Guilds:* a nationwide women's organization.
12 *Nikolaus Pevsner:* a well-known writer on architecture.
16 *R A F:* abbreviation for Royal Air Force.
50 *flogging:* selling (slang).

30

Sunday's TV

BBC 1   1

9 00–9 25 Apna Hi Ghar Samajhie.
For immigrants

9 30 Advances in Language Teaching

10 00 ¡Vamos a Ver!   5

10 30 Sung Eucharist

11 30 In Your Own Words

12 00 Engineering Design

12 30–1 00 Management Techniques

1 50–2 15 Farming; Weather   10

2 30 *Cluff: The Daughters*

3 20 Film Matinee: *The Remarkable Andrew* (American
film, 1942) starring William Holden. A ghost helps
a young book-keeper after city funds are stolen

4 40 *It's a Knockout*. Inter-town contests of skill and   15
strength: Galashiels *v*. Hawick

5 25 *Further Adventures of the Musketeers*. Part 2: *Treason*

5 50 Tich and Quackers

6 05 News; Weather

6 15 Meeting Point   20

6 45 Sunday Story

6 50 Songs of Praise

7 25 *Daddy Long Legs* (American musical, 1955) starring
Fred Astaire, Leslie Caron. A middle-aged playboy
falls for a young French girl   25

9 25 News; Weather

9 35 *Champion House*. Story of a wealthy Yorkshire
family. Starring Edward Chapman, Nicole Maurey

10 25 Red Army Spectacular. The Soviet Army Ensemble

11 15 Weather   30

11 17 Meeting Point

Title *TV*: abbreviation for television.

5 *¡Vamos a Ver!*: ('Let's see!', *Spanish*) a series of television programmes teaching Spanish.

14 *book-keeper*: a person who keeps the accounts of a firm or government department.

24 *playboy*: a wealthy man interested only in enjoying himself.

London ITV

Programme announcement in a national paper, 1968

32 *ITV:* abbreviation for Independent Television.

31

Dissatisfied with WRCC Road-Cleaning Service

A suggestion that Holmfirth and Meltham Councils might
form a cleansing department of their own if the service
offered by the West Riding County Council did not improve was made at the meeting of Meltham Council on
Monday night by Clr R. C. Ashton.

Both councils have been complaining about the clearance
of leaves and dirt from roads and pavements within their
areas. A month ago Clr Ashton said that in some cases
pavements were inches deep in leaves from last autumn.
They were trodden into a sodden bulky mass and as soon
as the weather improved there would be a most unpleasant
smell.

'Their Job'

Clr Ashton said that even now a brush had still not been
put to work on the pavements.

The Highways Committee had met the Divisional
Highways Surveyor, who had suggested that the Meltham
Council's engineer and surveyor should provide him with
details of specific areas so that the matters could receive
the County Council's attention.

'It is not the duty of our surveyor to go chasing round
the district looking for West Riding pavements that are not
swept. It is their job, not ours,' said Clr Ashton.

He suggested that the West Riding County Council
should begin a rota and said that if it was beyond them to
cope with the situation it was time that Holmfirth and
Meltham got together and formed a cleansing department of
their own.

'We are paying far too much for a service we are not
getting,' he complained.

Vandalism

His proposal, seconded by Clr H. B. Dearnley, that they
should ask the West Riding Highways Committee to form
a rota system for the Meltham area was carried unanim-
ously.

The engineer had reported to the Public Health Committee details of vandalism committed in the district. The Chairman of the Council (Clr H. Bastow), commenting on vandalism to the lighting in Roods Footpath, said it seemed
40 to be happening about once a month and cost the Council £30 every time in repairs.

Huddersfield Weekly Examiner, 27 April 1968

3 *West Riding:* the county of Yorkshire is divided into three administrative districts called Ridings.
3 *County Council:* a group of elected men and women who are responsible for the local government of a county.
5 *Clr:* a shortened form of 'councillor', a member of a council.

32

1 We get so used to the matter-of-fact world in which we live that we tend to take it for granted. As you read this you think you know what kind of a person you are, what your name and address are, and what colour the binding of this
5 book is. You are sure that two and two are four, that gunpowder is made of charcoal, sulphur and saltpetre, and what the difference is between alternating and direct electric currents. Then one day, as you are washing your hands, you happen to glance into the mirror over the basin and a sudden
10 doubt will flash across your mind. 'Is that really me?' 'What am I doing here?' 'Who am I?'

Each one of us is so completely cut off from everyone else. How do you know that you are reading a book? The whole thing may be an illusion. How do you know that red is red?
15 The colour may appear to be blue to everyone else's eyes. Father Ronald Knox summarized these doubts in his celebrated limerick:

There once was a man who said, 'God
Must think it exceedingly odd
20 If he finds that this tree
Continues to be
When there's no one about in the Quad.'

A similar doubt, differently expressed, is inherent in the question whether a tree falling in the desert far from the
25 nearest man makes any sound.

The whole complex, interlocking system of science, which we discussed in the earlier chapters of this volume, depends on facts and measurements, all of which are perceived through one or other of our five senses and by this means brought to bear on our brains. There is no ultimate assur- 30 ance that our senses do not play false. Let us, however, ignore for the moment this suspicion of our own sanity and take it that we do indeed see things as they really are and read the same sense from the same set of letters tomorrow as we read today. Perhaps we can also ignore the fact that 35 the modern scientific belief, that the universe is a systematic logical place in which miracles do not happen and in which *every* observation, no matter how apparently strange and un- expected, can be fitted into some sort of systematic hypo- thesis, is merely an act of faith. This is, of course, the modern 40 scientific creed. But it is assumed and not proved to be true, nevertheless.

Magnus Pyke: *The Boundaries of Science* (Harrap, 1961; Penguin Books, 1963)

16 *Father Ronald Knox:* a Catholic philosopher and writer of detective stories.

33

A two-year-old racehorse or a herd of milch cows, an oil 1 portrait of your dog or your own Mary Quant creation, a child-high Pooh Bear or a Dalek-sized Dalek – these and many thousand prizes more have lured consumers to chase the fifty or so manufacturers' competitions so far staged in 5 1967.

For millions of consumers, competitions are an amazing enough diversion, making modest demands on the house- hold budget and even more modest demands on the intel- ligence, always tingling with the far-out possibility of a 10 bonanza. For a few ten thousands of addicts, competitions are an obsession, almost a way of life. For many manufac- turers and their advertising agents, competitions – along with premiums, coupons and all the other marketplace gimmicks – are, in the jargon, 'powerful selling tools'. 15

Last year, according to the latest annual survey by MS Incentives, a sales promotion and research consultancy, an estimated £1,220,000 in cash and prizes was passed out to competition winners. This, despite six months of squeeze,
20 was an increase of £225,000 on 1965. In any one month last year anything between twenty-five and sixty competitions were running almost simultaneously.

In the postwar years competitions have become a sophisticated industry, involving not only the manufacturers but their advertising agencies; a handful of new firms special-
25 izing solely in promotions; half a dozen or so 'competition consultants' who do the mechanical work of dealing with entries; and panels of judges which solemnly determine, say, whether it is more important that a cigarette is 'firm and
30 well packed' or is 'a fine satisfying smoke'. Between the givers and the getters is the weekly magazine *Competitors Journal*, which for nearly fifty years has been publicizing current competitions and offering tactical advice to contestants. The magazine's audience of about 250,000 prob-
35 ably includes all the country's competition addicts and a high proportion of every competition's winners. And ever eager to attach themselves to this body of keen contest chasers is a whole sub-industry of astrologers, lucky-charm sellers and self-styled tipsters, all promising instant success.
40 It is doubtful, however, whether the really successful contestants need a 'Romany Zodiac Ring specially selected from a luck-laden Gypsy jewel-casket' or 'the greatest advance made in Astrology for perhaps 3000 years – the production by a computer of runs of lucky numbers that
45 *you were born with*'. The really successful competitors know just what they are doing. They have the knack.

John Barr in *New Society*, 23 February 1967

2 *Mary Quant:* a well-known modern British fashion designer.
3 *Pooh Bear:* a character in *Winnie the Pooh*, a famous English children's book by A. A. Milne.
3 *Dalek:* a science-fiction robot in a popular children's television serial.
19 *squeeze:* a period in which a government discourages wage increases.
26 *promotions:* publicity schemes.

34

There are experimental ways of investigating stereotypes. One
of the most obvious is to ask a group of people what traits
characterize the Germans, the Italians, the Americans and
so forth. Results of such studies on the whole agree fairly
well with what might have been expected; there is considerable agreement between different people in any one nation
regarding the most characteristic traits of other nations.
There is even agreement between different nations; for
instance, the Americans and English agree with respect to
other groups, and even, though less markedly, themselves.
The Germans, for instance, are regarded as scientifically
minded and industrious by English and Americans alike;
they are also considered solid, intelligent, mathematical,
extremely nationalistic, efficient and musical by the Americans, and arrogant, aggressive and over-nationalistic by the
English. Italians are regarded as artistic, impulsive, passionate, quick-tempered, musical, religious, talkative, revengeful, lazy, unreliable and dirty by both. Negroes fare even
worse. They are considered to be superstitious, lazy, happy-
go-lucky, ignorant, ostentatious, musical, slovenly, unreliable, dirty and religious by both Americans and English.
The Irish do rather better. While they too are religious
and happy-go-lucky, they are also supposed to be quick-
tempered, witty, industrious, nationalistic, quarrelsome,
aggressive and pugnacious Jews are believed to be shrewd,
mercenary, industrious, intelligent, loyal to family, grasp-
ing, ambitious, sly and persistent. They are also credited
with being very religious. The Chinese, as one would have
expected, are looked upon with more favour by the English,
who consider them industrious, courteous, meditative, intelligent and loyal to their families, than by the Americans,
who consider them superstitious, sly, conservative, ignorant
and deceitful. The Japanese stereotype seems to have altered
considerably as a result of the war. Where pre-war they
were considered intelligent, progressive, industrious, shrewd
and meditative, they are now considered cruel, fanatic,
treacherous, though still imitative and industrious. Perhaps
a few more years will serve to restore them to their previous

status. Turks do rather badly; apparently they are cruel, treacherous, sensual, dirty, deceitful, sly, quarrelsome, revengeful and superstitious. They make up for this by being very religious. The French, needless to say, are sophisticated, talkative, artistic, passionate and witty, whereas the Russians are industrious, tough, suspicious, brave and progressive. The English consider themselves sportsmanlike, reserved, tradition-loving, conventional and intelligent; astonishingly enough, Americans agree, adding, however, that the English are also sophisticated, courteous, honest, industrious, extremely nationalistic, and, I hardly dare put this down, humourless! The Americans consider themselves industrious, intelligent, materialistic, ambitious, progressive, pleasure-loving, alert, efficient, straightforward, practical and sportsmanlike; the English agree that Americans are materialistic and pleasure-loving, but also consider them generous, talkative and, most widely used adjective of all, boastful.

The close agreement found in English and American groups is probably due to the fact that these stereotypes derive from books, films and other cultural media shared by both groups. It is unlikely that a comparison between stereotypes held by Spaniards, Turks or Russians would show much agreement with those given here. To judge by German writings, it appears that, to the Germans, the average Englishman is 'a clever and unscrupulous hypocrite; a man who, with superhuman ingenuity and foresight, is able in some miraculous manner to be always on the winning side; a person whose incompetence in business and salesmanship is balanced by an uncanny and unfair mastery of the diplomatic wiles; a cold-blooded, prescient, ruthless opportunist; a calculating and conceited egoist.' There is little resemblance between this picture of the Englishman, quoted from an account by Harold Nicolson, and another one given by him. 'The French portrait of the Englishman is a picture of an inelegant, stupid, arrogant and inarticulate person with an extremely red face. The French seem to mind our national complexion more than other things. They attribute it to over-consumption of ill-cooked meat (O tempora! O mores!). They are apt, for this reason, to regard us as

barbarians and gross. Only at one point does the French
picture coincide with the German picture. The French share   80
with the Germans the conviction of our hypocrisy . . .'

H. J. Eysenck: *Uses and Abuses of Psychology,* (Penguin
Books, 1953)

72 *Harold Nicolson:* an English writer and critic.
77 *O tempora! O mores!:* What times! What habits! (*Latin*)

35

Let us pause to consider the English,   1
Who when they pause to consider themselves they get all
   reticently thrilled and tinglish,
Because every Englishman is convinced of one thing, viz:
That to be an Englishman is to belong to the most exclusive 5
   club there is:
A club to which benighted bounders of Frenchmen and
   Germans and Italians et cetera cannot even aspire to
   belong,
Because they don't even speak English, and the Americans   10
   are worst of all because they speak it wrong.
Englishmen are distinguished by their traditions and cere-
   monials.
And also by their affection for their colonies and their
   contempt for their colonials.   15
When foreigners ponder world affairs, why sometimes by
   doubts they are smitten,
But Englishmen know instinctively that what the world
   needs most is whatever is best for Great Britain.
They have a splendid navy and they conscientiously admire 20
   it,
And every English schoolboy knows that John Paul Jones
   was only an unfair American pirate.
English people disclaim sparkle and verve,
But speak without reservations of their Anglo-Saxon   25
   reserve.
After listening to little groups of English ladies and gentlemen at cocktail parties and in hotels, and Pullmans, of
   defining Anglo-Saxon reserve I despair,

30 But I think it consists of assuming that nobody else is there,

And I shudder to think where Anglo-Saxon reserve ends when I consider where it begins,

Which is in a few high-pitched statements of what one's
35 income is and just what foods give one a rash and whether one and one's husband or wife sleep in a double bed or twins.

All good young Englishmen go to Oxford or Cambridge and they all write and publish books before their grad-
40 uation,

And I often wonder how they did it until I realized that they have to do it because their genteel accents are so developed that they can no longer understand each other's spoken words so the written word is their only
45 means of inter-communication.

England is the last home of the aristocracy, and the art of protecting the aristocracy from the encroachments of commerce has been raised to quite an art,

Because in America a rich butter-and-egg man is only a
50 rich butter-and-egg man or at most an honorary LL.D of some hungry university, but in England why before he knows it he is Sir Benjamin Buttery, Bart.

Anyhow, I think the English people are sweet,

And we might as well get used to them because when
55 they slip and fall they always land on their own or somebody else's feet.

Ogden Nash: 'England Expects', from *The Face is Familiar* (Dent, 1954)

11 *because they speak it wrong:* 'wrong' here is US usage; in Britain people would say 'wrongly'.

22 *John Paul Jones:* a Scottish pirate and slave-trader who became Commodore of the American Navy during the War of Independence.

49 *butter-and-egg man:* a prosperous businessman (colloquial).

50 *LL.D:* (abbreviation for 'legum doctor', *Latin*), Doctor of Laws – a postgraduate degree in law. Here, the reference is to honorary degrees which occasionally used to be given by poor universities in return for a grant of money.

52 *Bart:* (shortened form of baronet) the most junior of English hereditary titles.

36

Soul and Understatement

Foreigners have souls; the English haven't.

On the Continent you will find any amount of people who sigh deeply for no conspicuous reason, yearn, suffer and look in the air extremely sadly. This is soul.

The worst kind of soul is the great Slav soul. People who suffer from it are usually very deep thinkers. They may say things like this: 'Sometimes I am so merry and sometimes I am so sad. Can you explain why?' (You cannot, do not try.) Or they may say: 'I am so mysterious ... I sometimes wish I were somewhere else than where I am.' (Do not say: 'I wish you were.') Or: 'When I am alone in a forest at night-time and jump from one tree to another, I often think that life is so strange.'

All this is very deep: and just soul, nothing else.

The English have no soul; they have the understatement instead.

If a Continental youth wants to declare his love to a girl, he kneels down, tells her that she is the sweetest, the most charming and ravishing person in the world, that she has *something* in her, something peculiar and individual which only a few hundred thousand other women have and that he would be unable to live one more minute without her. Often, to give a little more emphasis to the statement, he shoots himself on the spot. This is a normal, week-day declaration of love in the more temperamental Continental countries. In England the boy pats his adored one on the back and says softly: 'I don't object to you, you know.' If he is quite mad with passion, he may add, 'I rather fancy you, in fact.'

If he wants to marry a girl, he says:

'I say ... would you? ...'

If he wants to make an indecent proposal:

'I say ... what about ....'

Overstatement, too, plays a considerable part in English social life. This takes mostly the form of someone remarking: 'I say ...' and then keeping silent for three days on end.

George Mikes: *How to be an Alien* (Deutsch, 1956; Penguin Books, 1966)

1   Positioning the lips is a problem that recurrently challenges
the ingenuity of the embalmer. Closed too tightly, they tend
to give a stern, even disapproving expression. Ideally, em-
balmers feel, the lips should give the impression of being
5   ever so slightly parted, the upper lip protruding slightly for
a more youthful appearance. This takes some engineering,
however, as the lips tend to drift apart. Lip drift can sometimes be remedied by pushing one or two straight pins
through the inner margin of the lower lips and then insert-
10   ing them between the two front upper teeth. If Mr Jones
happens to have no teeth, the pins can just as easily be
anchored in his Armstrong Face Former and Denture
Replacer. Another method to maintain lip closure is to
dislocate the lower jaw, which is then held in its new
15   position by a wire run through holes which have been
drilled through the upper and lower jaws at the midline.
As the French are fond of saying, *il faut souffrir pour être
belle*.

If Mr Jones has died of jaundice, the embalming fluid
20   will very likely turn him green. Does this deter the embalmer? Not if he has intestinal fortitude. Masking pastes
and cosmetics are heavily laid on, burial garments and
casket interiors are colour-correlated with particular care
and Jones is displayed beneath rose-coloured lights. Friends
25   will say, 'How well he looks.' Death by carbon monoxide,
on the other hand, can be rather a good thing from the embalmer's viewpoint: 'One advantage is the fact that this
type of discolouration is an exaggerated form of a natural
pink colouration.' This is nice because the healthy glow is
30   already present and needs but little attention.

The patching and filling completed, Mr Jones is now
shaved, washed and dressed. Cream-based cosmetic, available in pink, flesh, suntan, brunette and blond, is applied to
his hands and face, his hair is shampooed and combed (and,
35   in the case of Mrs Jones, set), his hands manicured. For the
horny-handed son of toil special care must be taken; cream
should be applied to remove ingrained grime, and the nails
cleaned. 'If he were not in the habit of having them mani-

cured in life, trimming and shaping is advised for better
appearance – never questioned by kin.'

Jones is now ready for casketing (this is the present par- 40
ticiple of the verb 'to casket'). In this operation his right
shoulder should be depressed slightly 'to turn the body a
bit to the right and soften the appearance of lying flat on the
back.' Positioning the hands is a matter of importance, and
special rubber positioning blocks may be used. The hands 45
should be cupped slightly for a more lifelike, relaxed appearance. Proper placement of the body requires a delicate
sense of balance. It should lie as high as possible in the
casket, yet not so high that the lid, when lowered, will hit
the nose. On the other hand, we are cautioned, placing the 50
body too low 'creates the impression that the body is in a
box'.

Jones is next wheeled into the appointed slumber room
where a few last touches may be added – his favourite pipe
placed in his hand or, if he was a great reader, a book 55
propped into position. (In the case of little Master Jones a
Teddy Bear may be clutched.) Here he will hold open house
for a few days, visiting hours 10 a.m. to 9 p.m.

Jessica Mitford: *The American Way of Death* (Hutchinson,
1963; Penguin Books, 1965)

17 *il faut souffrir pour être belle:* you must suffer to be beautiful
(*French*).

38

JENNY: What do Ronnie say to it? 1
BEATIE: He don't mind. He don't even know though. He
ent never bin here. Not in the three years I known him.
But I'll tell you [*she jumps up and moves around as she talks*]
I used to read the comics he bought for his nephews and 5
he used to get riled – [*Now* BEATIE *begins to quote Ronnie,
and when she does she imitates him so well in both manner and
intonation that in fact as the play progresses we see a picture
of him through her.*] 'Christ, woman, what can they give
you that you can *be* so absorbed?' So you know what 10
I used to do? I used to get a copy of the *Manchester*

61

Guardian and sit with that wide open – and a comic behind!

JIMMY: *Manchester Guardian?* Blimey Joe – he don' believe in hevin' much fun then?

BEATIE: That's what I used to tell him. 'Fun?' he say, 'fun? Playing an instrument is fun, painting is fun, reading a book is fun, talking with friends is fun – but a comic? A comic? for a young woman of twenty-two?'

JENNY [*handing out meal and sitting down herself*]: He sound a queer bor to me. Sit you down and eat, gal.

BEATIE [*enthusiastically*]: He's alive, though.

JIMMY: Alive? Alive you say? What's alive about someone who can't read a comic? What's alive about a person that reads books and looks at paintings and listens to classical music?

[*There is a silence at this, as though the question answers itself – reluctantly.*]

JIMMY: Well, it's all right for some, I suppose.

BEATIE: And then he'd sneak the comic away from me and read it hisself!

JENNY: Oh, he didn't really mind then?

BEATIE: No – 'cos sometimes I read books as well. 'There's nothing wrong with comics' he'd cry – he stand up on a chair when he want to preach but don't wanna sound too dramatic.

JIMMY: Eh?

BEATIE: Like this, look. [*Stands on a chair.*] 'There's nothing wrong with comics only there's something wrong with comics all the time. There's nothing wrong with football, only there's something wrong with *only* football. There's nothing wrong with rock 'n' rolling, only God preserve me from the girl that can do nothing else!' [*She sits down and then stands up again, remembering something else.*] Oh yes, 'and there's nothing wrong with talking about the weather, only don't talk to me about it!' [*Sits down.*]

JENNY: He never really row with you then?

BEATIE: We used to. There was a time when he handled all official things for me you know. Once I was between jobs and I didn't think to ask for my unemployment benefit. *He* told me to. But when I asked they told me I was short on stamps and so I wasn't entitled to benefit. *I* didn't know what to say but he did. He went up and argued for me – he's just like his mother, she argues with everyone – and I got it. I didn't know how to talk, see, it was all foreign to me. Think of it! An English girl born and bred and I couldn't talk the language – except for to buy food and clothes. And so sometimes when he were in a black mood he'd start on me. 'What can you talk of?' he'd ask. 'Go on, pick a subject. Talk. Use the language. Do you know what language is?' Well, I'd never thought before – hev you? – it's automatic to you isn't it, like walking? 'Well, language is words,' he'd say, as though he were telling me a secret. 'It's bridges so that you can get safely from one place to another. And the more bridges you know about the more places you can see!'

Arnold Wesker: *Roots*, from *The Wesker Trilogy* (Penguin Books, 1959; Cape, 1960)

3 *ent never bin here:* hasn't ever been here (dialect).

11 *Manchester Guardian:* a quality daily newspaper now known simply as the *Guardian*.

13 *Blimey:* a mild oath, sometimes 'cor blimey', an abbreviation of 'God blind me'.

14 *hevin':* having (dialect).

20 *bor:* boy, person, man (dialect).

20 *gal:* girl (dialect).

41 *rock 'n' rolling:* a dance popular in the 1950s.

49 *unemployment benefit:* money paid to the unemployed by the Ministry of Social Security.

51 *stamps:* a reference to the contributions paid towards a worker's National Insurance in the form of stamps stuck each week into his insurance card.

39

' . . . I want photographs, Hawthorne.'

'That's asking a lot, sir.'

'We have got to have them. At any risk. Do you know what Savage said to me? I can tell you, it gave me a very nasty nightmare. He said that one of the drawings reminded him of a giant vacuum cleaner.'

'A vacuum cleaner!' Hawthorne bent down and examined the drawings again, and the cold struck him once more.

'Makes you shiver, doesn't it?'

10 'But that's impossible, sir.' He felt as though he were pleading for his own career. 'It couldn't be a vacuum cleaner, sir. Not a vacuum cleaner.'

'Fiendish, isn't it?' the Chief said. 'The ingenuity, the simplicity, the devilish imagination of the thing.' He re-
15 moved his black monocle and his baby-blue eye caught the light and made it jig on the wall over the radiator.

'See this one here six times the height of a man. Like a gigantic spray. And this – what does this remind you of?'

Hawthorne said unhappily, 'A two-way nozzle.'

20 'What's a two-way nozzle?'

'You sometimes find them with a vacuum cleaner.'

'Vacuum cleaner again. Hawthorne, I believe we may be on to something so big that the H-bomb will become a conventional weapon.'

25 'Is that desirable, sir?'

'Of course it's desirable. Nobody worries about conventional weapons.'

'What have you in mind, sir?'

'I'm no scientist,' the Chief said, 'but look at this great
30 tank. It must stand nearly as high as the forest-trees. A huge gaping mouth at the top, and this pipe-line – the man's only indicated it. For all we know, it may extend for miles – from the mountains to the sea perhaps. You know the Russians are said to be working on some idea – something to do with
35 the power of the sun, sea-evaporation. I don't know what it's all about, but I do know this thing is Big. Tell our man we must have photographs.'

Graham Greene: *Our Man in Havana* (Heineman, 1958; Penguin Books, 1958)

23 *H-bomb:* shortened form of hydrogen bomb.

40

Dear Daddy,

You really want to know what our problems are? Why we protest, love in, sit down, drop out, get high, rave or simply misbehave? You ask what we are really protesting about? Yet to ask what youth is protesting about is a silly question. It deserves, and often gets, the reply: 'What is everyone else complacent about?' The pressing question I should have thought, is not what, but what now? For there are as many reasons for protest as there are protesters.

I see you are all looking for universal causes of our frustration or dissatisfaction. But the universal answers turn out to be universally facile and universally unconstructive. The permissive society gets the blame, but no one knows precisely who, where or what it is. The generation gap is invoked, but those who believe in its existence also seem to believe in its inevitability, if not its necessity in the order of things. I think it exists to give the middle-aged something to protest about. Every specialist has got specialized answers. When we march, the politicians march with us. When we smoke pot, the doctors study us. When we drop out, the sociologists cluster round. Their views, I'm sure, are to be respected. But they are speaking about us, not for us.

There *is* a gap that I'm aware of, but it's so big you may scarcely see. It's an ideological gap, which means you and I will use different words for the same thing. We will adopt different priorities for the same problem and make different interpretations of the same situations. Above all, we will come up with different answers to the same questions. I don't see there is a hope in hell of your seeing it our way. I'd rather you didn't try, as a matter of fact, because if there's one thing worse than ignorant censure, it's ignorant admiration. And we've had enough of that heaped on us this year . . . .

I suppose of all prejudices, age-prejudice is one of the most crippling, matching disillusion with idealism, experience against enthusiasm. It makes so few distinctions, equates protest with delinquency, drop-outs with failure. It obscures the fact that everywhere the protests are continuing, articulate, organized and educated, and that we no

longer feel hopelessly determined by history. It ignores the
40 fact that every drop-out (your catch-phrase, I think, not
ours) is in fact society's failure. That each one of them is
concerned with the quality of life, which the stay-ins are in
no position to come to terms with. Active or passive,
though, we aren't deliberately trying to make things in-
45 sufferable for society. We are simply trying to be a constant
reminder that society *is* insufferable.

My Dear Sally,
    It must be very satisfying to know you're right. It's a
luxury I've not indulged in for many years now. There's a
50 confession for you – I probably seem to have spent the last
eighteen years pronouncing infallibly on what is right and
what is wrong. Well, I wonder how many times you caught
the lack of conviction in my voice? Not often probably.
Eighteen years of repetition is a long time to cultivate a
55 passable air of authority.
    You are right though, about the distorting effects of age-
prejudice. I appreciate that at forty-one, I may not be your
kind of scene, but I would certainly resent being classified
as a middle-aged archetype, as much as you would resent
60 being called a rocker or a teenybopper. However, just to
make the position clear, there are one or two prejudices I'd
like to get off my chest first. For a start I find your mumbo-
jumbo of sacred texts quite incoherent, and I refuse to be
blamed for not bringing you up a Hindu or a Buddhist.
65 We had our gurus, too, in our time, but we had to make do
with Marx as our revolutionary instead of Bolivian guerrillas,
whose jungle tactics you must surely find pretty irrelevant
in Hyde Park? If they are the keystone of your ideological
gap, I'd be very disappointed. I had always assumed it was
70 made of more original stuff. . . .
    What you might not have noticed is that you are begin-
ning to act out the stereotypes they have created. If, as you
say, we have become the slaves to affluence, you run the risk
of becoming slaves to your image. Television creates all
75 things to its own image, after all, and unless your generation
is aware of what makes you different from other generations,
you are all in danger of becoming irrelevant, of just stewing

in your 'expanding consciousness'. Which would be a pity.

If I tell you how I see it, feel free to reject this explanation along with all the others. No one pretends that parent–child conflicts haven't always existed. The king must die, after all, and the old must lose power, but will also struggle to retain it against the demands of the young. The conflict was cyclic, for by the time a man achieved power he was old himself and the cycle recommenced. The new factor is sociological. Affluence has brought with it the realization that you adolescents are a market. You have been exploited and in the process your 'teenage' image was created. The exploiters suffered the fate of Frankenstein – their creation developed a will of its own. You have begun to disseminate not the ideas embodied in the exploiters' concepts, but your own ideas.

So this is the new factor. The young have gained a class-consciousness, in the Marxian sense. Your demands are not for Coke and candies as the exploiters hoped, but for social change; this social change is not just for you, to be exchanged in time for the key of the door, but for all of us. So the cycle is ending. You have, to continue the analogy, taken over from the discredited proletariat the role of the revolutionary class. As one of your more garrulous spokesmen puts it, I believe, you should not be trying to destroy government and authority, but to make it redundant.

I think perhaps you understand all this instinctively. But do you understand us? We are used to thinking that recovery from adolescence was usually spontaneous. It was a great comfort. Now we see you, the first planned generation, with television in your blood and radioactivity in your bones, and we wonder if any of us will recover.

Michael Wynn-Jones in *Nova*, December 1968

2 *love in:* to join a gathering of young people demonstrating the need for tolerance and understanding (slang).

2 *sit down:* to make a protest against war or a social injustice by sitting down and staying there until moved by the police (slang).

2 *drop out:* to refuse social responsibilities (slang).

2 *get high:* to become elated under the influence of drugs (slang).

19 *pot:* the drug marijuana (slang).

57 *I may not be your kind of scene:* I may not belong to your way of life (slang).

60 *rocker:* member of a gang wearing jeans and leather jackets and riding powerful motor cycles.

60 *teenybopper:* children between about ten- and fourteen-years-old distinguished by sophisticated clothes and attitudes far in advance of their age (US slang).

65 *guru:* originally a Hindu word for a teacher; now used for any spiritual or intellectual guide or mentor.

66 *Bolivian guerrillas:* a reference to Ché Guevara, an Argentinian doctor and revolutionary theorist, who was a leading figure in the Cuban Revolution and who died organizing a revolution in Bolivia in 1967.

89 *Frankenstein:* a fictional scientist who created an artificial monster.

106 *the first planned generation:* a reference to the fact that birth control did not become widely accepted in Britain until after the Second World War.

41

1 What do you do with a kid who can't read, even though he's fifteen-years-old? Recommend him for special reading classes, sure. And what do you do when those special reading classes are loaded to the roof, packed because there are kids who
5 can't read in abundance, and you have to take only those who can't read the worst, dumping them on to a teacher who's already overloaded and who doesn't want to teach a remedial class to begin with?

What do you do with that poor ignorant jerk? Do you call
10 on him in class, knowing damn well he hasn't read the assignment because he doesn't know how to read? Or do you ignore him? Or do you ask him to stop by after school, knowing he would prefer playing stickball to learning how to read, and knowing he considers himself liberated the
15 moment the bell sounds at the end of the eighth period?

What do you do when you've explained something patiently and fully, explained it just the way you were taught to explain it in your education courses, explained it in minute detail, and you look out at your class and see that
20 stretching vacant wall of blank, blank faces, and you know nothing has penetrated, not a goddam thing has sunk in? What do you do then?

Give them all board erasers to clean.

What do you do when you call on a kid and ask, 'What did

that last passage mean?' and the kid stands there without 25
any idea of what the passage meant, and you know he's not
alone, you know every other kid in the class hasn't the
faintest idea either? What the hell do you do? Do you go
home and browse through the philosophy of education
books the GI Bill generously provided? Do you scratch 30
your ugly head and seek enlightenment from the educational
psychology texts? Do you consult Dewey?

And who the hell do you condemn, just who?

Do you condemn the elementary schools for sending a kid 35
on to high school without knowing how to read, without
knowing how to write his own name on a piece of paper?
Do you condemn the master minds who plot the educational
systems of a nation, or a state, or a city?

Do you condemn the kids for not having been blessed
with IQs of 120? Can you condemn the kids? Can you 40
condemn anyone? Can you condemn the colleges that give
you all you need to pass a Board of Education examination?
Do you condemn the Board of Education for not making
the exams stiffer, for not boosting the requirements, for not
raising salaries, for not trying to attract better teachers, for 45
not making sure their teachers are better equipped to teach?

Or do you condemn the meatheads all over the world
who drift into the teaching profession, drift into it because it
offers a certain amount of pay-cheque-every-month security,
vacation-every-summer luxury, or a certain amount of 50
power, or a certain easy road when the other more difficult
roads are so full of ruts?

Evan Hunter: *The Blackboard Jungle* (Constable, 1955;
New English Library, 1967)

9 *jerk:* fool (US slang).

12 *to stop by:* to stay in (US usage).

13 *stickball:* a street game played by American children.

30 *GI Bill:* A bill which gave government funds to ex-soldiers in the
United States so they could complete their education or professional
training.

32 *Dewey:* John Dewey, a well-known American educational
philosopher and writer.

40 *IQ:* (abbreviation for Intelligence Quotient) the scale used to
measure human intelligence; 100 is taken as the average.

47 *meatheads:* fools (US slang).

42

1 So you think we're street preachers and tambourine bangers.
We're proud of it.

We're also the largest independent social service organization in Britain. And nobody ought to be proud of that.

5 *Why We're in the Social Service Business*

The fact is that the Welfare State just cannot reach far enough. There are people who have to rely on charity simply to live. Not a pretty thought in this day and age, is it?

10 There are deserted wives with children who just exist in appalling squalor. There are thousands of old people who have no one to look after them. There are unmarried mothers shattered by anxiety. There are misfits and alcoholics who would die in the gutter. Some do.

15 We know how hard it is to reach a man's soul if he's got an empty stomach. We've been saying that for a hundred years now. And for a hundred years we've been feeding and housing the edge of humanity: the people you never see, never hear about.

20 There are 193 social service establishments operated by the Salvation Army in Britain: sixty-one homes and hostels for men, thirty-one homes and hostels for women and girls, thirteen maternity homes and two maternity hospitals, thirty-eight old people's homes, four children's homes, and 25 others.

That's just not enough. There are still people sleeping on streets who would rather have a bed. There are still old people dying alone and unwanted, sometimes helpless and ill. Husbands desert wives every day. Criminals are released 30 every day, rootless, friendless, jobless and homeless. New alcoholics hit bottom every day, more teenagers go wrong every day. The Salvation Army is better trained and better equipped than ever, but to our alarm, the need is actually increasing.

35 So over the next few months, we're going to show you the sort of people we help everyday, in the hope that their plight will persuade you to give us a pound.

Where your £ Will Be Spent

The money raised with this campaign is to be spent entirely in Britain. We need three million pounds to build new homes, hostels, clinics, and to buy new equipment.

Trained Social Workers

The Salvation Army Officer is a professional. He (or she) devotes his life to helping others. He has spent two years at the Army's training school for officers at Camberwell, London. You can be sure your money will be wisely and carefully spent.

What You Can Do

Just give us a pound. Or more if you can spare. Please clip and post this coupon with your cheque or money order. We'll send you back a 'Salvation Bond'. It's our way of saying we promise to use your money well. And of saying thanks.

For *God's* sake care,
give us a pound.

```
Dear Salvation Army _____
something must be done _____
Here's £_____
Name _____
Address _____
Post to Dept 24, 101 Queen Victoria Street, London, EC4
```

Salvation Army advertisement in National Press, May 1967

6 *Welfare State:* the comprehensive network of Government social services.

21 *Salvation Army:* a religious organization founded in the nineteenth century for social work among criminals and the underprivileged.

43

My mother's relations were very different from the Mitfords. Her brother, Uncle Geoff, who often came to stay at Swinbrook, was a small, spare man with thoughtful blue eyes and

a rather silent manner. Compared to Uncle Tommy, he was
an intellectual of the highest order, and indeed his vitriolic
pen belied his mild demeanour. He spent most of his waking
hours composing letters to *The Times* and other publications
in which he outlined his own particular theory of the development of English history. In Uncle Geoff's view, the
greatness of England had risen and waned over the centuries in direct proportion to the use of natural manure, or
compost, in fertilizing the soil. The Black Death of 1348
was caused by gradual loss of the humus fertility found
under forest trees. The rise of the Elizabethans two centuries later was attributable to the widespread use of sheep
manure.

Many of Uncle Geoff's letters-to-the-editor have fortunately been preserved in a privately printed volume called
Writings of a Rebel. Of the collection, one letter best sums
up his views on the relationship between manure and freedom. He wrote:

Collating old records shows that our greatness rises and falls with
the living fertility of our soil. And now, many years of exhausted
and chemically murdered soil, and of devitalized food from it, has
softened our bodies and still worse, softened our national character. It is an actual fact that character is largely a product of the soil.
Many years of murdered food from deadened soil has made us
too tame. Chemicals have had their poisonous day. It is now the
worm's turn to re-form the manhood of England. The only way
to regain our punch, our character, our lost virtues, and with
them the freedom natural to islanders, is to subsoil and compost
our land so as to allow moulds, bacteria and earthworms to re-
make living soil to nourish Englishmen's bodies and spirits.

The law requiring pasteurization of milk in England was a
particular target of Uncle Geoff's. Fond of alliteration, he
dubbed it 'Murdered Milk Measure', and established the
Liberty Restoration League, with headquarters at his house
in London, for the specific purpose of organizing a counter-
offensive. 'Freedom not Doctordom' was the League's
proud slogan. A subsidiary, but nevertheless important,
activity of the League was advocacy of a return to the 'un-
split, slowly smoked bloater' and bread made with 'English

stone-ground flour, yeast, milk, sea salt and raw cane-sugar.'

Jessica Mitford: *Hons and Rebels* (Gollancz, 1960)

7 *The Times:* the best-known quality daily newspaper in Britain.

44

For one reason or another, this year's Royal Film, *The* 1
Taming of the Shrew, is bound to start more excitement than
usual when it opens in London tomorrow. The chief reason
is, of course, that the film has been directed by that brilliant
Shakespearean anarchist, Franco Zeffirelli. 5

To get a clear and concise idea of how it was done we
consulted Michael York, the young actor who plays
Lucentio. He seemed well qualified on various grounds.

He watched events with a fresh eye because the *Shrew*
was his first experience in films. He was in Zeffirelli's 10
National Theatre production of *Much Ado* about which
there was that fuss when it was moved over to TV. Moreover, Michael York has already proved his own competence
in his second film, *Accident,* which by accident appeared in
London first and goes on general release today. 15

'Working with Zeffirelli,' he says, 'is like having a holiday.
There's a sense of positive enjoyment. He's like a Renaissance extrovert. There's always an element of surprise.

'He'll say: "First we do this scene for an English
audience" and it's very traditional, very classical. "Now 20
we'll do it for Italians," he says – and we were all kissing
and throwing our arms in the air and . . . barmy. All the
time Zeffirelli knows exactly what he wants.

'The set in Rome was like an antique shop. All the
costumes were made by lots of little old ladies in a Florentine 25
dressmaker's. He hand-picked the extras. He knew them all.

'Some came from a village south of Rome, full of light-
skinned Italians imported by Mussolini from the north – a
very inbred village. But Zeffirelli ranged everywhere. His
own aunt, the Burton children, the *capelloni* ("the long- 30
haired ones") who hang about the Spanish Steps – he put
them all in tights.

'There's a marvellous excitement working for him. "Silence!" he shouts. Everyone trembles. Then "Azione!"
35 and – ricochet – we were off. I loved it.'

'Briefing' in the *Observer*, 26 February 1967

1 *Royal Film:* a film chosen in Britain each year to be shown before the Royal Family; the money from this performance goes to charity.
5 *Franco Zeffirelli:* an Italian theatre and film director.
11 *Much Ado:* Shakespeare's play, *Much Ado About Nothing.*
12 *TV:* abbreviation for television.
28 *Mussolini:* head of state in Italy from 1922 to 1943.
34 *Azione!:* Action! (*Italian*).

45

Directions
Mixing
1 Always add *Polyfilla* to water. For average indentations and small cracks add two parts *Polyfilla* to one part of water. On very absorbent surfaces and for deep cracks and holes use stiffer mix – less water. Mix thoroughly. Prepare as much as
5 you need – *Polyfilla* will stay workable for approx. one hour. Keep the mixing vessel clean, as old set plaster or *Polyfilla* will shorten the setting time. When mixing, you can colour *Polyfilla* by adding some paint. When using distemper mix some of the distemper with the *Polyfilla.*

10 ### Applying
To walls, ceilings, joints in plaster boards, making good round gas or hot water pipes, etc. Simply brush out cavities, and cracks. Press in *Polyfilla* firmly with a filling knife or trowel to fill the crack completely, then smooth off. The
15 positive adhesive bond of *Polyfilla* needs no additional anchorage, so that you do *not* have to cut back or enlarge the crack. Do not wet in. For large deep-seated cavities use an economical mixture of two parts *Polyfilla* to one part sand.
20   Behind doors, windows, skirting boards, between floor-boards, making good chased-in pipes, plugging walls for lightweight domestic fixtures and electric light switches,

etc. *Polyfilla* is ideal for use in all places where vibration would dislodge ordinary plaster fillers. Its cellulose adhesive bond to plaster, brick and wood keeps it firmly in position – *Polyfilla* simply will *not* shake loose or fall out. 25

For cracks behind sinks, washbasins, etc. You can use *Polyfilla* as a putty for *damp places* behind *kitchen sinks*, *bathrooms* and for *exterior work*. Prepare *Polyfilla* as for 30 a Swedish putty. Apply oil paint or varnish over *Polyfilla* after drying.

All woodwork. Apply *Polyfilla* direct before priming or painting. Fill joints, cracks, knot holes, screw and nail holes; plug cut-outs of removed hinge plates, locks and 35 handles. Do not damp woodwork before filling. Simply press *Polyfilla* well into the cracks and holes. Nail-heads unless of a non-rusting nature should be touched with paint before applying *Polyfilla*. For wood grain filling, add more water till *Polyfilla* is of a creamy thickness. 40 Brush on.

Directions for *Polyfilla*, Polycell Products Ltd, Welwyn Garden City, Herts

5 *approx.*: shortened form of approximately.
11 *making good*: repairing.
16 *cut back*: clear out loose material from a hole in a plaster wall.
17 *wet in*: moisten a hole before filling with plaster.
21 *chased-in pipes*: pipes set into grooves to make them level with the surrounding wall.
31 *Swedish putty*: a putty made with linseed oil.
35 *cut-outs*: shallow depressions where door hinges, etc. are fitted.

46

But to get back to advertising. The same day as I was not 1 tempted to flog cars in Vietnam, I saw a different kind of advert, an advert for adverts. Such adverts can also be revealing.

It was in *Advertisers Weekly*, and was for a publication 5 called *Holidays Galore*, which promised advertisers a circulation of five million to upper-class, middle-class and upper-working-class homes only.

It even went further and promised 'not a single copy in
the wrong sort of home'.

If you are not quite with it, brother, the wrong sort of
home is one with not enough lolly. The advertising world
is a hard world. It knows such homes exist. Waffle from
Harold and George about incomes being too great, hence
the freeze, has never kidded it for one mean second.

So they've got us all pigeon-holed.

Some might claim the class war is dying, but the ad-men
have been hotting up social classes quite a profitable bit.

We are now all classified as either A, B, C1, C2, D or E–
depending on our occupations and incomes. The E folk
are pensioners and lower-paid workers with less than
£6 10s. a week. In the ad-world they're known as the
half-sack-of-coal and a-packet-of-processed-cheese-a-week
people.

D people are contemptuously thought likely to buy a
souvenir in Blackpool and cook steak in casseroles on
Sunday, on their £6 10s. to £14 a week.

C2 people are reckoned to buy cheap 'knowledge' books
on their doorsteps, have a second-hand car and blue fittings
in their bathrooms. All on £14 to £22 a week.

And so it goes on up the scale to A people, who are
reckoned by ad-men to be A1 people. They are supposed to
give to charity, keep poodles, send the kids to private
schools, take the *Express* and have full central heating.
Their incomes are put at £2000 plus.

But it's not all a matter of money. Clergymen are automatically AB men, although some may be poorer than their
own mice.

So the ad-men's national game of Grade Your Neigh-
bour is not all that simple. It's a matter, too, of whether
you have a cocktail cabinet which lights up (bad). Go
abroad for your holidays (good). Say toilet (bad). Have a
car plastered with I've-been-to-Frinton stickers (bad), or
live in Islington (good). Good, that is, if you are one of the
middle classes who have moved to Canonbury. Bad if you
are one of the working class born there.

It's a bad thing to be at the bottom of the consumer
heap, according to the ad-men. I can only think of one

thing worse than living in the 'wrong sort of home', that
would be to be Lower Middle Class – like most ad-men.   50

Bob Wynn in the *Morning Star*, 1 June 1967

2 *flog:* sell (slang).

11 *if you are not quite with it:* in case you don't quite understand
(slang).

11 *brother:* often used as an informal term of address, especially among
communists (the *Morning Star* is the official Communist newspaper in
Britain).

14 *Harold and George:* Harold Wilson, Prime Minister of the British
Labour government from 1964 to 1970, and George Brown, Foreign
Secretary in the same government until 1968.

15 *freeze:* a period of economic standstill when wage claims and prices
are meant to be 'frozen' (colloquial).

16 *pigeon-holed:* classified into appropriate categories.

17 *ad-men:* advertising men; people who plan and write for advertising
campaigns (colloquial).

28 *'knowledge' books:* encyclopedias sold on the doorstep by travel-
ling salesmen.

34 *take the Express:* read the *Daily Express*, a popular newspaper.

43 *Frinton:* a seaside resort.

44 *Islington:* a district in London.

45 *Canonbury:* a fashionable section of Islington.

47

Overtaking

Never overtake unless you *know* that you can do so without   1
danger to yourself or others. Be specially careful at dusk
and in fog or mist, when it is more difficult to judge speed
and distance.

Overtake on the Right   5

This rule does not necessarily apply in the following
circumstances:

1. When the driver in front has signalled his intention to
turn right and you can overtake him on his left without
inconveniencing other traffic, or when you are filtering to   10
the left at a junction.

2. In slow-moving congested traffic when vehicles in the
lane on your right are moving more slowly than you are.

Return to the appropriate lane on the road as soon as
practicable after overtaking, but do not cut sharply in   15
front of the vehicle you have just overtaken.

Do not overtake at or when approaching
    a pedestrian crossing
    a road junction
20   a corner or bend
    the brow of a hill
    a hump-back bridge
Do not overtake
    where the road narrows
25   where the road is marked with double white lines and the line nearer to you is continuous if this would involve crossing the continuous line
    when to do so would force another vehicle to swerve or reduce speed
30   *If in doubt – hold back*

The Highway Code (Her Majesty's Stationery Office, 1970)

13 *lane:* a road with three lanes is one wide enough for three cars to move forward side by side.

48

Billy Graham's Advice to UN

1   Billy Graham, the all-American evangelist, was back in town yesterday, bashing the Bible at London's Waldorf Astoria Hotel for the greater enlightenment of the Press and, he hoped, the United Nations.

5   'God has a very interesting passage here in this prophecy: "In that day shall Israel be third with Egypt and Syria, even a blessing in the midst of the land."'

Physically he is type-cast for Burt Lancaster playing Elmer Gantry, suntanned, lean and rangy, clean-cut, with
10 an irresistible Southern voice which deepens and darkens like sherry rolled around a glass when he wants to stress a point.

The first point that he wanted to stress yesterday was that the best brains in the Security Council should be
15 studying the writings of God, in the Books of the Prophets, to find a solution to the Middle East situation. 'There are literally hundreds of passages about the area. Some of

them are symbolical, but many of them are literal, and I think the text usually shows quite plainly which is which.'

But on Vietnam, about which God, unfortunately, has not written, Dr Graham refused to be drawn. 'I've found that the American people don't like their citizens to comment on American foreign policy while abroad.'

He also refused to say whether he thought England's need for the 'relevance, simplicity and authority of God' was greater than Canada's whence he has just come, or that of Italy and Yugoslavia, where he preaches next month.

'I don't want to be involved in an international moral battle: that could be worse for me than Vietnam.'

He did volunteer views on safer subjects. He thinks that if the posters in New York's Times Square are anything to go by then 'American movies are certainly dirtier than ever'. He knows that 'all sexual relationships outside marriage, in any age, in any circumstances, are wrong and we mustn't be afraid to say so'.

Dr Graham, who is here with ten associate evangelists, says he feels that if there could be a great spiritual renaissance in Britain it would 'sweep the world'.

The Billy Graham All Britain Crusade organizers are doing their best to make this happen. True, Dr Graham hasn't got the facilities he will have later this year in Tokyo, when he is looking forward to preaching the gospel to the entire Japanese people on television, through an interpreter. . . .

He also has his eye on some less likely converts. He told us of the president of the 'far, far left' Humanities Club at Columbia who had written to him: 'Doctor Graham, we do not accept your beliefs. We are professing atheists. But we are haunted by the figure of Jesus.' Many people when they were young felt that it was novel to be atheistic, but as they grew older they had to come to terms with Christ – 'Your Mr Muggeridge even'.

Mary Holland in the *Observer*, 18 June 1967

Title *UN*: abbreviation for United Nations.
2 *bashing the Bible*: preaching (US slang).
8 *type-cast*: when an actor is chosen for a part which matches his

personality or physical appearance, as here, or for a part like others he has often played.

8 *Burt Lancaster:* an American film star.

9 *Elmer Gantry:* the hero in a novel and film of the same name.

14 *Security Council:* the United Nations body responsible for keeping international peace.

46 *'far, far left':* revolutionary in their political thinking.

47 *Columbia:* an American university.

52 *Mr Muggeridge:* Malcolm Muggeridge, an English writer and television personality.

49

1   There was the business of the fagcards. We all collected them as a matter of course. I had no dad to pass them on to me and Ma smoked some awful cheap brand that relied on the poverty of its clients rather than advertisement. No one
5   who could have afforded anything better would have been content to smoke them. This is the only feeling of inferiority I can trace right back to the Row but it was strictly limited; not that I had no dad, but just that I had no fagcards. I should have felt the same if my parents had been married
10 non-smokers. I had to rely on pestering men in the streets.
    'Got a fagcard, mister?'

    I liked fagcards; and for some reason or other my favourites were a series of the kings of Egypt. The austere and proud faces were what I felt people should be. Or do I
15 elaborate out of my adult hindsight? The most I can be certain of is that I liked the kings of Egypt, they satisfied me. Anything more is surely an adult interpretation. But those fagcards were very precious to me. I begged for them, bargained for them, fought for them – thus combining
20 business with pleasure. But soon no one with any sense would fight me for fagcards because I always won.

    Philip commiserated, rubbed in my poverty; pointed out the agony of my choice – never to have any more kings of Egypt or else exchange those I had for others and thus lose
25 the first ones for good. I toughed Philip up mechanically for insolence but knew he was right. The kings of Egypt were out of my reach.

    Now Philip took the second step. Some of the smaller

boys had fagcards which were wasted on them. What a
shame it was to see them crumpling kings of Egypt they   30
were unable to appreciate!

I remember Philip pausing and my sudden sense of
privacy and furtive quiet. I cut right through his other
steps.

'How we going to get 'em?'   35

Philip went with me. Immediately I had jumped to the
crux, he adapted himself to my position without further
comment. He was elastic in such matters. All we – he said
we, I remembered that clearly – all we had to do was to
waylay them in some quiet spot. We should then remove   40
the more precious cards which were of no use to them.
We needed a quiet place. The lavatory before school or
after school – not in break time, he explained. Then the
place would be crowded. He himself would stand in the
middle of the playground and give me warning if the   45
master or mistress on duty came too near. As for the
treasure, for now the cards had become treasure and we
pirates, the treasure should be divided. I could keep all
the kings of Egypt and he would take the rest.

William Golding: *Free Fall* (Faber, 1959)

1 *fagcards:* picture postcards given away inside packets of cigarettes.
Fag is a slang term for a cigarette.
7 *the Row:* the nickname of the street where the boy narrator lived.
25 *toughed up:* beat someone up (slang).

50

I believe that every parent in this country who understands   1
the problem of teachers' salaries is on our side in the
campaign for higher pay.

Unfortunately, however, many parents do not yet see the
connexion between the standard of education provided for   5
their children and the salaries offered to teachers. They
seem to think the same teacher will be there no matter
what the salary.

But the truth is that in many areas a confidence trick is being played on parents. They send their children to school believing they are taught by a qualified teacher, when in fact the children are taught by an unqualified person and are getting an indifferent education.

If parents found out that when they sent a child to the doctor he was attended to by an unqualified person there would soon be an outcry. Of course, they can go to a doctor with confidence. But so far as our profession is concerned, local authorities are prepared to appoint untrained people. If parents were aware of all the implications, something would happen very quickly.

They should be aware that without a substantial increase in teachers' pay which will attract large numbers of able people to our profession, the nation cannot carry out planned reforms in education.

The NUT wants to see:

Implementation of the *Plowden Report* to bring about a big improvement in primary schools.

Raising of the school-leaving age.

A reduction in the size of classes.

Reorganization of secondary education on comprehensive lines.

These are some of the tasks before the nation. Yet already the manpower resources of our schools are stretched to breaking point. Moreover, people are constantly leaving the profession – not only married women but men teachers too.

Young people come into the education service with a vast amount of idealism. Then, at the start of their careers, they find themselves with a salary which makes life almost impossible.

Teachers 'Rationed'

They cannot work near home because teachers are 'rationed' among local authorities and are forced to live away at much greater expense. It does not require much imagination to see how difficult it is to live on a wage of £14 a week gross and about £10 or £11 net. It means a very low standard of living.

Some teachers train for primary or secondary schools but prefer to go into colleges or the private sector, attracted by higher salaries. Some go to teaching posts overseas paid 50 for by our own Government – in places where there are Service families, for example. This depletes our own primary and secondary schools.

My union's recent Annual Conference urged the removal of discrimination against teachers in primary schools due 55 to what is called the 'points' system. This is a device which determines how head teachers will be paid and what other extra salary payments will be available. Under this system, children in the primary schools are considered less important than others and count fewer 'points'. This device 60 has been a grievance in the teaching profession for years and its removal is of special importance in view of the *Plowden Report* on the primary schools. If the report's proposals are to be implemented we must attract high-quality people in large numbers to primary education. 65

Less Attractive

If this part of our system, however, provides the least amount of elbow room so far as promotion prospects are concerned, the ablest and most ambitious teachers will look elsewhere. At present the primary school is relatively 70 less attractive from the point of view of promotion prospects, yet the primary schools have led the way in educational thinking and practice. At our Conference the Education Minister, Mr Anthony Crosland, paid tribute to the primary schools – to the better relationship between child 75 and teacher, the improved art and craft work and the lifted standards of reading.

Friends from abroad have told me they find our primary schools most exciting places and in my lifetime there has been a complete change in the attitude of children to school. 80 The idea that a child creeps unwillingly to school is completely out of date. Children want to go to school. The primary schools, in fact, have become a revolutionary part of our education system.

Teachers in all schools want to give every child the 85 opportunity of benefiting from the advances which have

taken place in education. They want to give children much more individual attention. But ours is a vastly under-manned industry. If we are to attract people in the numbers
90 required, something substantial and dramatic must be done so far as salaries are concerned.

This is not a straight economic question. It involves the future well-being of children and of society itself. It involves your children. That is why it should matter to you.

95 Sir Ronald Gould's address to parents: National Union of Teachers leaflet (May 1967)

25 *NUT:* abbreviation for National Union of Teachers.

26 *Plowden Report:* a government report (1967) recommending various changes in primary education.

30 *comprehensive:* in the educational sense as here: to educate all the children from a district in a single school, rather than separating them into academic and non-academic schools on the basis of an intelligence test at the age of eleven.

43 *local authorities:* the Department of Education and Science is responsible for all education in England and Wales, but schools and colleges are actually run by local education authorities.

45 *a wage of £14 a week gross:* the starting wage (before tax is paid) of a teacher who is trained, but has not been to university.

52 *Service:* belonging to the Army, Navy or Air Force.

81 *creeps unwillingly to school:* a reference to Shakespeare's *As You Like It*, Act 2 Scene 7: '. . . the whining school-boy with his satchel/And shining morning face, creeping like a snail/Unwillingly to school.'

51

1 The rejection of Labour by the voters of London was not a clear verdict on their rule. Boredom, apathy and national resentment dominated it. It was hardly the result of an evaluation of their thirty-three years of power.

5 To evaluate those years and their achievement is a complex business. Probably the simplest way for a Londoner is to look about and judge his city for himself.

Labour ruled during years that were as formative for this city as those that followed the Great Fire. It was seldom
10 dramatic rule, for drama played little part in the LCC and will do less in the GLC. This was the most workaday of

public institutions and the extent of its power and influence was almost unknown.

It was created in 1899 out of a welter of uncoordinated authorities. Its birth created no enthusiasm. London was made a county, but for this metropolitan county there was no civic splendour, no stately hospitality, no tradition, not even, at first, a coat of arms. It was a county without the traditional gentry to serve it. It was from the first severely practical and almost unattractively austere in its behaviour. It has kept to this local tradition. . . .

Its first Chairman was Lord Rosebery and it divided between Progressives and Moderates. But the London Labour Party was founded in 1914 and in the next year Herbert Morrison was made its part-time secretary at £1 per week. A bouncy fierce little man with a stabbing finger and an arrogant quiff of hair across his forehead. This party came to power in 1934.

It was a proud moment for Labour which had never known real power and had suffered a calamitous election defeat three years before. It marked a milestone – this capture of the largest city in the world – on Labour's road to national power. It was also the beginning of a remarkably long lease of power in London.

The symbols of those thirty-three years are all around. Most of them are the fruit of victories in old, forgotten battles. One of the most striking is the new Waterloo Bridge. Herbert Morrison took a crow-bar to start the demolition of Rennie's narrow masterpiece across the Thames and it was done in the face of Governmental and public disapproval.

There was the clearing of the South Bank, done by a deal with Morrison, who was then in the Cabinet as Lord President of the Council, when the LCC persuaded him to use the site in preference to Battersea Park. There are hundreds of night schools which were clear expressions of Labour ideology and which now teach anything from guitar playing to bee-keeping. It built up a remarkable system of education. . . .

Its members were and are unpaid, though they can claim some expenses. All of them had to have private

means, or a job that allowed them the time for London's work. It required devotion and a certain selflessness and it paid back with none of the prestige of Parliament across
55   the river, which is a far less efficient institution.

Now it is the Greater London Council and its extent has been increased and its powers diminished. It looks after nearly eight million people and covers an area extending from Enfield in the north to Croydon in the south,
60   from Hounslow in the West to Romford in the east. One in every six British voters comes within its reach.

Patrick O'Donovan in the *Observer*, 16 April 1967

1 *Labour:* one of the two major political parties in Britain.
1 *voters of London:* a reference to local government elections for the Greater London Council.
9 *the Great Fire:* a famous fire which destroyed half of London in 1666.
10 *LCC and GLC:* abbreviations for London County Council, and its successor the Greater London Council.
39 *Rennie:* a famous nineteenth-century architect.
44 *the Council:* the Privy Council, a committee of eminent men who advise on some State affairs.

52

1   The treatment accorded the Negro during the Second World War marks, for me, a turning point in the Negro's relation to America. To put it briefly, and somewhat too simply, a certain hope died, a certain respect for white
5   Americans faded. One began to pity them, or to hate them. You must put yourself in the skin of a man who is wearing the uniform of his country, is a candidate for death in its defence, and who is called a 'nigger' by his comrades-in-arms and his officers; who is almost always given the
10   hardest, ugliest, most menial work to do; who knows that the white GI has informed the Europeans that he is sub-human (so much for the American male's sexual security); who does not dance at the USO the night white soldiers dance there, and does not drink in the same bars white
15   soldiers drink in; and who watches German prisoners of war being treated by Americans with more human dignity

than he has ever received at their hands. And who, at the
same time, as a human being, is far freer in a strange land
than he has ever been at home. Home! The very word
begins to have a despairing and diabolical ring. You must 20
consider what happens to this citizen, after all he has
endured, when he returns – home: search, in his shoes, for
a job, for a place to live; ride, in his skin, on segregated
buses; see, with his eyes, the signs saying 'White' and
'Coloured', and especially the signs that say 'White 25
Ladies' and 'Coloured *Women*'; look into the eyes of his
wife; look into the eyes of his son; listen, with his ears, to
political speeches, North and South; imagine yourself
being told to 'wait'. And all this is happening in the richest
and freest country in the world, and in the middle of the 30
twentieth century. The subtle and deadly change of
heart that might occur in you would be involved with the
realization that civilization is not destroyed by wicked
people; it is not necessary that people be wicked but only
that they be spineless. 35

James Baldwin: *The Fire Next Time* (Michael Joseph, 1963;
Penguin Books, 1964)

11 *GI:* a nickname for American soldiers, which comes from the
abbreviation of the words 'General Issue' stamped on American
army equipment.
13 *USO:* (abbreviation for 'United Services Organization') provides entertainment and club facilities for Americans serving in the
armed forces.

53

The next motion was an obvious one and it was made by 1
the tall, slender Bonaro, quickly seconded by two other
eager voices. There was about the proponents of the
motion an eagerness to meet any opposition but the committee was in no mood to re-hear the arguments put forth. 5
If it had to be done it would be best done swiftly. Ed
Shotwell barely paused for any discussion but plunged at
once into the voting. The voting now left Arthur in a
curiously naked position. His was the only vote cast against
the motion to rescind the invitation to Larry Isler – the 10

Marcuses abstained and Bud Davis voted for. When the lushly formed Mrs Bunetta read the final count the solitary vote cast against fell with the disconcertingly sharp sound of a coin dropped in a marble vault. It seemed to call for an explanation but Arthur remained silent. It was Bud Davis who finally rose.

'I think Mr Douglas has every right in the world to vote against it, and I'll tell you right now I was mighty tempted to vote against the motion myself. I was tempted because I realize that we have put Mr Douglas into a very curious position. He extended that invitation in good faith to Mr Isler. He extended it believing that this was the intention of the committee. I don't know if he could have foreseen that the committee would be against inviting Mr Isler. I don't know how much truth there is in the things Mr Bunetta and Mr Bonaro and the others have said. I don't doubt them, understand. I believe that they spoke up in good conscience and good faith. And I believe that Mr Douglas defended his choice in good conscience and good faith. But, after all, the interests of the library come first and I think you would all agree that the good interests of the library would not be best served by having a controversial figure here as a guest of the committee. Mr Isler, as I've said, may or may not be what Mr Bunetta and the others say he is. But we've certainly had abundant evidence that, whatever he is, he *is* a controversial figure and so wouldn't be a good choice for us. But nevertheless I believe Mr Douglas deserves a vote of thanks from this committee and I, for one, propose that right now.'

'And I second it!' said Marcus, springing up.

'Well, ah, I don't suppose there's any need for discussion on that motion,' said Ed Shotwell with a faint smile, 'and I suppose you all feel that it ought to be unanimous. . . .'

'Just a moment,' Arthur said, rising. 'Before your vote of thanks is officially entered in the minutes of this meeting I think you ought to know what I think of your thanks— and most of you.' Arthur caught the sick smile on some of their faces, a smile of uneasy anticipation. 'I will pass over the insult you have given to Mr Isler. I don't think he

88

will be much disturbed by it since he will never have the
need of meeting any of you face to face. You certainly don't
qualify as members of his intellectual or social circle and
a man can't really be insulted by his inferiors.' Arthur
looked at them coldly. 'And you are certainly his inferiors   55
in every connotation of the word. But what sickens and
disgusts me is that I have shown the abysmal lack of good
taste and good judgement to become associated with you.
You are possibly the most dreary collection of slack-jawed,
vacuous yahoos it has ever been my bad luck to meet. I   60
don't know what sins against the human spirit and the
intellect can be excused on the grounds of neighbourliness
and civic pride, but however many there are, I've gone
over my quota tonight. Those of you who aren't cowards
are bigots and those who aren't bigots are sheep and some   65
of you are all three. I demeaned myself by standing before
you and treating you as though you were my equals. I won't
make that mistake again, I assure you. Now get out of my
house.'

Arthur turned on his heel and walked off the patio into   70
the house.

David Karp: *Leave Me Alone* (Gollancz, 1958; Penguin
Books, 1965)

1 *motion:* here, proposal.

54

MR CALLAGHAN: There has been a great deal of emotion,   1
not all of it of the purest kind, expressed about the problem,
and I can only say that the statement that was issued by
the Conservative Party yesterday, and which I read with
very great care, in many ways goes along with the state-   5
ment I have made today. We have both been thinking no
doubt on similar lines. I have had a great deal of time to
think about that and I would hope – and here I address
this particularly to the Honourable Gentleman – that we
would not get into a party controversy about this and that   10
there will be no inflammatory statements made.

MISS LESTOR: Would my Right Honourable Friend not

agree that the agitation and the racialist statements which
have been made by the Right Honourable Member for
15 Streatham [Mr Sandys] and the Honourable Member for
Louth [Sir C. Osborne] over the last few years have produced what they wanted – the acceleration of immigrants
from Kenya and other parts of the world which has forced
us into a position that is abhorrent to many of us on this
20 side of the House?

MR CALLAGHAN: This is asking me for an opinion. If I
am asked for it, I will give it. It seems to me that three
factors have contributed to the situation over the last few
months. The first is the action of the Kenya Government
25 in relation to employment; the second the action of
the Kenya Government in relation to trading facilities for
these people; and thirdly the speeches of some Right
Honourable Gentlemen opposite.

MR HOGG: Does the Right Honourable Gentleman realize
30 that it is extremely important to keep the temperature
down about this kind of thing and that attacks on individuals in this House on either side do not necessarily
help us to do so?

MR CALLAGHAN: I follow that, but I think we ought to
35 understand that a great deal of agitation among East
African Asians has been caused by suggestions here that
there is going to be closure of the immigration controls,
and that this has precipitated a flow which would not
otherwise have been as great as it will be now.

40 MR MACDONALD: Is there any precedent for restricting the
right of holders of British passports to enter this country,
and are we to understand that holders of British passports
are to be restricted whereas residents of Eire will be able
to enter quite unrestricted?

45 MR CALLAGHAN: This is a unique situation. There has
been no precedent for it, as far as I know. This will be the
first occasion on which legislation of this sort has been pro-
posed. The position of Eire citizens is different.

MR THORPE: Could I press the Home Secretary a little
50 further on the question raised by my Honourable Friend
the Member for Roxburgh, Selkirk and Peebles [Mr
David Steel]? The Right Honourable Gentleman has

said that this is the first time that holders of United Kingdom passports may be excluded from coming into the United Kingdom. My Honourable Friend has asked whether this was to be a matter which would be subject to an independent appeal. The Home Secretary said that he had not funds to do that and that the Wilson Report had not recommended it. Surely the Right Honourable Gentleman should have independent and impartial machinery for judging the claims of United Kingdom passport holders who are excluded from coming to this country? Is it not a reasonable request . . . .

[*Several Honourable Members rose.*]

MR SPEAKER: Order. We are going to debate this on Tuesday.

MR SANDYS: In view of the fact that I was personally attacked by the Honourable Lady for Eton and Slough [*Miss Lestor*] – [*Interruption*].

MR SPEAKER: Order. We should be able to proceed.

MR SANDYS: I wonder whether I might be allowed an additional supplementary question?

MR SPEAKER: I do not see why not, in the circumstances.

MR SANDYS: Thank you, Mr Speaker. In view of the remarks made by the Honourable Lady the Member for Eton and Slough and possibly, by implication, although I do not know, by the Home Secretary about my speeches recently, may I ask the Home Secretary whether he realizes, that at the request of his predecessor, I remained silent on this question for over a year and that it was only when the flood of immigrants from East Africa started that I felt it necessary to speak out?

MR SPEAKER: Order. We shall debate this issue on Tuesday.

MR ST JOHN-STEVAS: On a point of order. Unless you, Mr Speaker, were referring to the Right Honourable and Learned Member for St Marylebone as 'Mr St John-Hogg', did I not hear you call my name?

MR SPEAKER: It sometimes happens that half a backbencher's name is called and then his being called is preempted by a Front Bench Member. This is most unfortunate. I called half the Honourable Gentleman's name.

MR ST JOHN-STEVAS: Could I ask half my supplementary
question?

95 MR SPEAKER: I knew that it was not an innocent point of
order.

Debate on Commonwealth Immigration: *Hansard* (vol. 759,
no. 66, 22 February 1968)

9 *Honourable Gentleman:* traditional way of addressing Members of
Parliament during Parliamentary sittings.

19 *This side of the House:* Government and Opposition seats are opposite each other in the House of Commons.

49 *Home Secretary:* the Minister in charge of the Home Office, the
government department in Britain responsible for home affairs.

65 *Mr Speaker:* the Chairman of the House of Commons is known as
the Speaker.

84 *On a point of order:* a method of formally drawing attention to an
irregularity of procedure.

88 *backbencher:* in the House of Commons, those members who do
not hold a ministerial post sit on the benches at the back of the chamber.

55

1   I was having a wash down at the bathroom sink, when up
came the Hoplite, nervously patting his hair which was done
in a new style of hair-do like as if a large animal had licked
the Hoplite's locks down flat, then licked the tip of them

5   over his forehead vertical up, like a cockatoo with its crest
on back-to-front. He was wearing a pair of skin-tight,
rubber-glove-thin, almost transparent cotton slacks, white
nylon-stretch and black wafer-sole casuals, and a sort of
maternity jacket, I can only call it, coloured blue. He looked

10 over my shoulder into the mirror, patting his head and saying nothing, till when I said nothing too, he asked me,
'Well?'

'Smashing, Hoplite,' I said. 'It gives you a rugged shaggy
Burt Lancaster appearance.'

15 'I'm not so sure,' the Hoplite said, 'it's me.'

'It's you, all right, boy. Of course, anything is. Fabulous.
You're one who can wear *anything*, even a swimsuit or a
tuxedo, and look nice in it.'

'I know you're one of my fans,' the Hoplite said, smiling
sadly at me in the mirror, 'but don't mock.'   20

'No mockery, man. You've got dress sense.'

The Hoplite sat down on the lavatory seat, and sighed.
'It's not dress sense I need,' he said, 'but horse sense.'

I raised my brows and waited.

'Believe it or not, my dear,' the Hoplite continued sadly,   25
'but your old friend Fabulous, for the first time in his life –
the *very* first time in nineteen years (well, that's a lie, I'm
twenty really) – is deep, deep, deep in love.'

'Ah,' I replied.

There was a pause.   30

'You're not going to ask me with who?' he said appeal-
ingly.

'I'm so sure you're going to tell me, Hop.'

'Sadist! And not *Hop* please!'

'Not me. No, not a bit, I'm not. Well – who is it?'   35

'An Americano.'

'Ah'.

'What does this "Ah" mean?' the Hoplite said sus-
piciously.

'Several things. Tell me more. I can see it coming, though.   40
He doesn't care.'

'Misery! That's it.'

'Doesn't care for the angle, Hoplite, or doesn't care for
you personally, or just doesn't care for either?'

'The angle. Not bent at all, though I had hopes that   45
perhaps he dabbled.... And he's so, so understanding,
which makes it so, so, so much worse.'

'You poor old bastard,' I said to the Hoplite, as he sat
there on my john, almost crying.

He plucked at a piece of sanitary tissue, and blew his nose.   50
'I can only hope,' he said, 'it doesn't turn me anti-Ameri-
can.'

Colin MacInnes: *Absolute Beginners* (MacGibbon & Kee,
1959)

8 *casuals:* shoes for informal wear.
13 *smashing:* fine, I like it (slang).
14 *Burt Lancaster:* an American film star.
45 *bent:* here, homosexually inclined, usually dishonest (slang).
49 *john:* lavatory (U S slang).

1 The Eagle Tower is the finest of all the towers, and is part of the work of 1285–94. In 1300 it is called the Great Tower, and its foundations were damaged by the sea in that year. It is first called the Eagle Tower in 1316, and it is
5 evident that a great deal of work was done to it at this time. The roof was being leaded in 1316–17, when the tower is described as having been made anew. A stone figure of an eagle was set on the Great Tower in April 1317.

10 The origin of the name of the tower is not certain. An eagle occurs on the first seal of the town of Caernarvon, of late thirteenth-century date, above the leopards of England. Otho de Grandison, Constable at this time, bore eagles in his arms, and it is also to be remembered that the Honour of
15 the Eagle was annexed to the Crown by Henry III in 1268, granted to Prince Edward, afterwards Edward I, in 1269, and remained with the Crown till 1373.

The tower was evidently much damaged in 1294, and its repair was postponed on account of the new buildings in the
20 outer court; indeed it seems to have been left until all the other towers had been repaired. In 1343 it still had five camina unfinished. There are five fireplaces in the tower, of which at least three must have been completed as the walls rose, so that the reference may be to the octagonal chimney
25 shaft rising above the wall tops.

The tower is ten-sided in plan, the walls being fifteen feet thick at the ground floor, while the internal diameter at this level is thirty-four feet. In the top floor it is thirty-six feet, owing to the setting back of the wall faces. The floors and
30 ceilings of these large rooms were carried on huge oak beams supported by struts from corbels, the modern beams which replace them giving a very good idea of their effect, though if the beam holes in the wall are to be trusted, the old beams were slightly larger than those now seen. The new floors and
35 roof date from 1911–14. The tower is of four stages, the lowest being a basement reached by a flight of steps from the court, and opening to the quay by a postern door on the west.

Caernarvon Castle: *Official Guide* (Ancient Monuments and
Historic Buildings, Her Majesty's Office of Works, 1961)

22 *camina:* a room in a medieval castle.

31 *corbels:* a projection built out from a wall to act as a support for
floor, roof, etc.

37 *postern door:* a small side door into a castle often used as a means of
quiet unseen exit, or for unexpected attack on an enemy concentrated
in front of the main gate.

57

My First Meeting with Elgar
Yehudi Menuhin

For me the Elgar Concerto will always hold more meaning   1
than a purely musical one, in that it evokes a less universal
and a more specific atmosphere, one composed of people I
love, of places which call forth the roots of my life, a youthful atmosphere of years which must appear to most of us as   5
though in a nostalgic candlelight compared with the in-
human and merciless glare of contemporary life.

This particular association is surely not just my own, for I
feel I share it with the British people and with those of my
own generation who hear this music in the same spirit of   10
comfortable surrender as when one settles into the trusted
and familiar folds of a beloved armchair.

I well remember the sunny day when I first made my
acquaintance with the infinitely shaded green of an English
summer and with Sir Edward, who to me symbolized in one   15
way the country I had come to love.

We met in an hotel room where HMV had already arranged for Mr Ivor Newton to play the piano reduction for
me as accompaniment. I played a few bars in a mood at once
eager and anxious, for I had just prepared the work and I   20
was presenting it, after all, to the composer himself.

I had scarcely reached the end of the first page when Sir
Edward interrupted, saying that he had no qualms about the
performance and that he was sure the recording would be
excellent – and as for him – he was off to the races!   25

I was terribly impressed as I had never met so trusting

and casual a composer! Of course I came to realize how much lay behind this cultivated air of detachment, how much warmth, feeling and intensity were at work within the
30 unruffled frame of the English, both individually and collectively.

It was therefore of particular sentiment to me that HMV should choose to commemorate the one-hundredth anniversary of Elgar's birth by bringing out anew on a long
35 play record this version of the violin concerto recorded in my mid-teens with Sir Edward.

I really feel it would be redundant for me to dissect the work or to discuss it technically for the benefit of the English public. Is it not sufficient to say that for me it presents some-
40 thing so intrinsically English in its charm and persuasive lyrical beauty that, as I felt in those far-off days with Elgar, the music is a language we share, one that needed then no especial translation between himself and myself, any more than it does now between myself and the English audience?
45 For me it is the vocal expression of a bond that I have felt since I first played for them, and as such is more articulate than any words I might find to explain it.

Yehudi Menuhin: cover notes for EMI Record (ALP 1456), written for the centenary issue of the Elgar Violin Concerto in B Minor, Opus 61

Title *Elgar:* Sir Edward Elgar (1857–1934), English composer.
    Yehudi Menuhin: a famous violinist; born in Hungary, now naturalized English.
    17 *HMV:* abbreviation for His Master's Voice, a recording company.
    18 *Ivor Newton:* a famous English pianist, specializing in accompaniments.
    18 *piano reduction:* piano part or score arranged from the music for the whole orchestra.

58

Review by the Chairman
The Metal Box Company Limited

1 Review by the Chairman, Lord Kings Norton, for the year ended 31 March 1967.

I referred last year to my retirement this year under the rules governing the retirement of executive directors. I look forward to taking the chair at the Annual General Meeting on 20 July. At the end of that meeting I intend to retire from the chairmanship and from the Board. My successor as Chairman is, as foreshadowed in my 1966 review, Mr David Ducat, to whom I offer my best wishes. I am deeply grateful to him and my other colleagues on the Board and on the staff for the support and help they have given me in my nine years with the company.

The performance of the company in the year which ended on 31 March last was in two respects remarkable. On the home front, in a time of economic stagnation, the company did extremely well. Abroad, hit by the devaluation of the rupee, the overseas company, whose progress in recent years has been spectacular, received a check. Adding the two sets of results produces sales of £145·8 million and a trading profit of £14·2 million. The sales figure, which is £4·4 million more than last year, would, had there been no devaluation in India, have been over £152 million. The net income of the company is £6·5 million compared with £6 million last year.

This year is the first to bear the full weight of the changes in the tax system which, in addition to the corporation tax of 40 per cent, require the income tax deducted from dividends distributed to be paid to the Exchequer.

Whilst the UK and overseas taxes have taken the same proportion of the profit as last year, the tax on dividends amounted to £1,912,000, which was £1,170,000 more than last year when only the tax on the final ordinary dividend was caught. This heavy drain on our cash is likely in time to be alleviated to some extent as the claims for investment grants are settled. It is estimated that these grants on expenditure to 31 March 1967 will be £1,258,000. This cash benefit is being credited to profit over the expected life of the relevant assets and in this year amounted to £98,000 ....

It looks as if our steady progress will continue at home and that we shall resume our advance overseas.

If the United Kingdom enters the Common Market your company is likely to benefit because there will be greater

opportunities both for us and for our customers to increase
exports to the Six.

45   The Annual General Meeting will be held on Thursday,
20 July 1967 at The Dorchester, Park Lane, London, W1
at 12 30 p.m.

Company Report in National Press, July 1967

26 *corporation tax:* a tax (at present 42½%) on profits of all companies.
This tax was introduced in 1965 to replace income and profits tax.
    41 *Common Market:* the economic alliance of six European countries.
    44 *the Six:* the six countries of the Common Market area.

59

1 **Lively professional** mixed group, Jewish, invites male
members aged 25–39. Meetings informal. Programme
varied. Please write to Delta Society, Box 4189.
Pesetas available for property development and purchase
5 in Spain. Box 4174.
The days are drawing out. Remember those that cannot
see the new green leaves and early flowers. Send a donation
to the Guide Dogs for the Blind Association, 83/89 Uxbridge
Road, Ealing, W5, or just add a line to your will.
10 **Alone on holiday?** Join Mrs Graham's specially planned
parties for the unattached to Spain, Italy, Majorca. Write
Vista Tours, 234 Tottenham Court Road, London, W1
Tel. LAN 5391.
Over 4,750,000 vivisection experiments still take place in
15 this country every year. Unwanted animals, strays, pets
stolen from good homes, are sold to laboratories by unscrupulous dealers at a good price. We save many helpless
animals from this 'black market', protect and find homes
for them. But our unceasing efforts need continuous volun-
20 tary financial support. Please help with a donation. The
National Anti-Vivisection Society Ltd, Dept O, 51 Harley
Street, W1.
For sale – Mellotron – 'An orchestra at your finger tips'.
Owner wishes to dispose of a *Mellotron*, virtually unused
25 and in perfect condition. This is the perfect instrument for
clubs, restaurants or home entertainment. £500 o.n.o.

Please contact Mrs R. W. Randall — Tel. 021-556-2161
(WED 2161) between 9 a.m. and 5 p.m.

'Ancestry tracing & genealogists'. Free from Institute
of Heraldic & Genealogical Studies, Northgate, Canterbury. 30

End bedwetting. Medically approved. No drugs. Write
Dri-Nite, 70 Nursery Road, N14.

Diary of a somebody. Fascinating exposé of the Group of
European beauties in Elliott Collection. Featuring the in-
nermost secrets of fashion-conscious women suffering from 35
narrow feet. Write to A. A. Elliott, Rede Place, London,
W2 for full coloured miniature diary. FREE.

Female, gentle, intelligent and refined to look after a boy
and girl aged 5 and 6, in Florence, Italy. Lovely villa on
hillside with private room and bath. Children are in school 40
from 9 a.m. to 5 p.m. for six days a week allowing governess
time for leisure, study or social life. Some housekeeping in
the children's area. Father a retired American physician
living permanently with them in Italy. Box 4190.

Advertisements in the *Observer*, 1969

  18 *black market:* illegal buying and selling.
  26 *o.n.o.:* abbreviation for 'or nearest offer'.

60

Rags (Wiping Rags) (Maximum Charges) (Amendment) Order, 1945

1. Basic charge means in relation to the services to which   1
this Order applies.

a. The charge made for such services in the ordinary course
of the business in the course of which those services were
being performed during the week beginning 31 August   5
1942, in accordance with the method of charge then in
being in relation to that business for performing such
services.

b. Or the charge made for such services in the ordinary
course of a substantially similar business during the said   10
week, in accordance with the method of charge then in being
in relation to that business for performing such services;
provided that in any case in which a person who performs

such services proves that such services were being per-
15 formed in the course of his own business during the said
week, 'basic charge' shall only have the meaning specified
in sub-paragraph (a) of this paragraph.

'Rags' means any worn-out, disused, discarded or waste
fabric or material made wholly or mainly from wool, cotton,
20 silk, rayon or flax or from any mixture thereof.

'Wiping rags' means rags each one of which is not less
than 144 square inches in size and has been trimmed and
washed and is suitable for use as a wiping rag.

This may provoke the comment that the washing of
25 wiping rags can hardly be worth such lavishness of words.
But that is beside the point. The point is that the law, whatever it is about, must be certain; and if it is necessary for the
law to concern itself with washing wiping-rags, it must be
no less certain here than anywhere else. If anyone thinks
30 that he can draft more simply and no less certainly, I advise
him to try his hand and then ask an expert whether he can
find any loopholes.

Ernest Gowers: *The Complete Plain Words* (Her Majesty's
Stationery Office, 1954; Penguin Books, 1962)

61

1 DOCTOR: There is a good deal of risk involved in – the
operation. . . .
MRS VENABLE: You said that it pacifies them, it quiets
them down, it suddenly makes them peaceful.
5 DOCTOR: Yes. It does that, that much we already know,
but . . .
MRS VENABLE: What?
DOCTOR: Well, it will be ten years before we can tell if the
immediate benefits of the operation will be lasting or –
10 passing or even if there'd still be – and this is what haunts
me about it! – a possibility, afterwards of – reconstructing
a – totally unsound person, it may be that the person will
always be limited afterwards, relieved of acute disturb-
ances but – *limited* – Mrs Venable . . .
15 MRS VENABLE: Oh, but what a blessing to them, Doctor, to
be just peaceful, to be just suddenly – peaceful . . . .

[*A bird sings sweetly in the garden.*]

After all that horror, after those nightmares: just to be able to lift up their eyes and see – [*she looks up and raises a hand to indicate the sky*] a sky not as black with savage devouring birds as the sky that we saw in the Encantadas, Doctor.

DOCTOR: Mrs Venable? I can't guarantee that a lobotomy would stop *babbling*!!

[*Pause : faint jungle music.*]

MRS VENABLE: That may be, maybe not, but after the operation, who would *believe* her, Doctor?

DOCTOR [*quietly*]: My God.

[*Pause.*]

Mrs Venable, suppose after meeting the girl and observing the girl and hearing this story she babbles – I still shouldn't feel that her condition's – intractable enough! to justify the risks of – I suppose I shouldn't feel that non-surgical treatment such as insulin shock and electric shock and –

MRS VENABLE: SHE'S HAD ALL THAT AT ST MARY'S!! Nothing else is left for her.

DOCTOR: But if I disagreed with you?

[*Pause.*]

MRS VENABLE: That's just part of a question: finish the question, Doctor.

DOCTOR: Would you still be interested in my work at Lion's View? I mean would the Sebastian Venable Memorial Foundation still be interested in it?

MRS VENABLE: Aren't we always more interested in a thing that concerns us personally, Doctor?

DOCTOR: Mrs Venable!!

[CATHARINE HOLLY *appears between the lace window curtains.*]

You're such an innocent person that it doesn't occur to you, it obviously hasn't even occurred to you that anybody less innocent than you are could possibly interpret this offer of a subsidy as – well, as a sort of *bribe*?

MRS VENABLE [*laughs, throwing her head back*]: Name it that – I don't care – there's just two things to remember. She's a destroyer. My son was a *creator*! Now if my honesty's shocked you – pick up your little black bag

without the subsidy in it and run away from this garden!
Nobody's heard our conversation but you and I, Doctor
Sugar . . .

60   [MISS FOXHILL *comes out of the house and calls.*]

MISS FOXHILL: Mrs Venable?

MRS VENABLE: What is it, what do you want, Miss Foxhill?

MISS FOXHILL: Mrs Venable? Miss Holly is here, with . . .

    [MRS VENABLE *sees* CATHARINE *at the window.*]

65 MRS VENABLE: Oh, my God. There she is, in the window!
. . . I told you I didn't want her to enter my house again.
I told you to meet them at the door and lead them around
the side of the house to the garden and you didn't listen.
I'm not ready to face her. I have to have my five o'clock

70 cocktail first, to fortify me. Take my chair inside. Doctor?
Are you still here? I thought you'd run out of the garden.
I'm going back through the garden to the other entrance,
Doctor Sugar? You may stay in the garden if you wish or
run out of the garden if you wish to or go in this way if

75 you wish or do anything that you wish to but I'm going to
have my five o'clock daiquiri, *frozen!* – before I face her . . .

    [*All during this she has been sailing very slowly off through
the garden like a stately vessel at sea with a fair wind in her
sails, a pirate's frigate or a treasure-laden galleon. The*

80   *young* DOCTOR *stares at Catharine framed by the lace
window curtains.* SISTER FELICITY *appears beside her
and draws her away from the window. Music: an ominous
fanfare.* SISTER FELICITY *holds the door open for*
CATHARINE *as the* DOCTOR *starts quickly forward. He*

85   *starts to pick up his bag, but doesn't.*]

CATHARINE: Excuse me.

DOCTOR: I'm sorry . . . .

    [*She looks after him as he goes into the house.*]

SISTER FELICITY: Sit down and be still till your family

90 come outside.

Tennessee Williams: *Suddenly Last Summer* (Secker &
Warburg, 1959; Penguin Books, 1961)

21 *the Encantadas:* a mountain range in Mexico.

23 *lobotomy:* a brain operation used in the treatment of people who
are mentally ill.

76 *daiquiri:* an iced drink made from rum, lime-juice and sugar.

No cricketer in England faces a harder task than the Nawab   1
of Pataudi, who has soon to lead an inexperienced Indian
team, without any fast bowlers, into a Test series. Some
people seem to know the result already; cannier ones keep
their silence for the moment, with a watchful eye on Pataudi   5
himself, who was not nicknamed 'Tiger' as a child without
due cause.

Up to a point Pataudi can be described in clichés. He is a
'leader born' and 'a man of many parts'. He really is somewhat 'inscrutable'. But it is as a man of surprises that he   10
strikes most forcibly. Suddenly one realizes that the lithe
young player from Winchester, Oxford and Sussex, though
only twenty-six, has had the experience of leading India in
as many as eighteen out of twenty-one Tests. With only a
blur of vision in his right eye, following a car accident in   15
1961, his batting and fielding depend to a remarkable extent
on quickness of sight and reflex. For those who have
counted Pataudi as part of the English cricket scene, it is
even a slight surprise to find how very Indian he feels.

Home is not in the southern counties, among the old   20
stones of Oxford, or in the Parks – to which he returned on
Saturday with a triumphant century and where yesterday
he sat ruefully watching the drizzle. Home is in New Delhi,
where he has business in real estate, in Hyderabad, for
whom he plays and where his two married sisters live, and   25
in Bhopal, where he was born. He may prefer steak in
England, but there was a time here when his Muslim
orthodoxy extended to avoiding ham – not easy on the
county cricket circuit. It seems characteristic that his main
interest outside cricket and work is Indian classical music,   30
which has lately caught the ear of people as far apart as
Yehudi Menuhin and the Beatles. Pataudi plays the *tabla*, a
percussion instrument of infinite subtlety.

There is an aristocratic cast to his aquiline face, intense
and rather severe, breaking out occasionally into a grin of   35
almost incongruous breadth. Nawab is roughly the Muslim
equivalent of the Hindu maharajah; he assumed the title
when his father, still warmly remembered as a player for

Oxford, Worcestershire, and both England and India, died
in 1952. The elder Nawab, as captain of his own country,
left his son a daunting challenge to live up to on the cricket
field, though political power is no more in the modern India.
There is still a farming concern in the small state of Pataudi,
but the present incumbent answers quite cheerfully to a
disrespectful 'Pat'.

Christopher Ford in the *Guardian*, 16 May 1967

1 *Nawab*: an Indian prince.
3 *Test series*: a series of cricket matches played between two national
teams.
12 *Winchester*: a famous English public school (a public school is, in
fact, a private school charging fees).
12 *Oxford*: the University of Oxford.
12 *Sussex*: a county in the south of England. Here, the reference is to
its cricket team.
21 *the Parks*: public parkland in the town of Oxford; the reference is
to the cricket ground there.
22 *century*: here, a score of 100 runs or more in cricket.
32 *Yehudi Menuhin*: a famous violinist.
32 *the Beatles*: a famous group of popular singers who compose many
of their own songs.

63

It is possible to gain a better understanding of attempted
suicide if we regard it as conveying a particular degree of un-
certainty that the attempt will succeed or fail. Attempts at
suicide are unlike successful suicides and they are made by
different people in different ways. The true goal of the
attempted suicide is not self-destruction but survival, without however losing the advantages of self-destruction. The
reverie which precedes the suicidal attempt contemplates
the possible consequences and concludes that suicide would
do more harm than good, and would therefore defeat its own
purpose, which is often to compel affection and esteem. The
distinction between attempted and successful suicide is borne
out by the fact that only a small proportion of those who
attempt suicide actually commit suicide subsequently, and
that only about 15 per cent of actual suicides have pre-
viously attempted suicide, although this proportion varies

somewhat from one investigation to another. Successful suicides occur more frequently among older people, among men, and among the unmarried, divorced or widowed. Attempts at suicide are more common among younger 20 people, among women and among the married.

Attempts at suicide, like Russian roulette, appear to be a gamble with death. Studies of preparations made for the attempt at suicide reveal that the person's psychological probability of death ensuing from his attempt may range 25 from near certainty that he will die to near certainty that he will live. He acts in this way because he does not wish to take upon himself the sole burden of making the fateful decision. Therefore he provokes 'fate' to make the decision for him. In a Danish investigation of 500 attempted suicides, 30 only about 4 per cent of the attempts were said to be well planned; some 58 per cent involved some danger to life, and 7 per cent of the attempts were considered to be more or less harmless. An example will illustrate this suicidal gamble. A man swallowed a large number of sleeping pills, telephoned 35 his wife and the police, and then sat down to wait for an ambulance. This was an attempt at suicide the outcome of which was uncertain and dependent on external circumstances. The telephone might have been engaged or the line might have been out of order. The pills could have exerted 40 a lethal effect before the ambulance arrived. The man was hazarding his life, but implicitly or explicitly he must have assessed the chances of being rescued.

John Cohen: *Chance, Skill and Luck* (Penguin Books, 1960)

22 *Russian roulette:* a game where one bullet is loaded into a revolver and, after the chamber has been spun round, the end is placed against the person's head and the trigger pulled, so the 'winner' loses.

64

Misplaced Minister

Last Friday at Cambridge it was Mr Denis Healey's turn 1 to face the turbulence of students. The Defence Secretary seems to have carried the whole thing off with the expected aplomb and good humour. Had it not been for the bright

5 lights and cameras inviting the students to perform, and
   for some characteristic mismanagement by the local police
   (who traditionally detest undergraduates), Mr Healey's
   visit might well have passed off with nothing worse than
   some ill-tempered, ill-mannered shouting. It was Mr
10 Patrick Gordon Walker, Secretary for Education and
   Science, who transformed the Cambridge incident into
   something of real political significance.

   Mr Gordon Walker chose to give a radio interview the
   next day, and told his interviewer:

15 People are becoming more and more conscious of the fact that
   the students are supported by the taxpayers. It is very grave.
   People know that students are very privileged people, but they
   behave as though they were totally underprivileged, or a small
   minority do.

20 In other words, the minister answerable for student affairs
   took the opportunity to re-emphasize the dislike, envy and
   fear aroused in too many people's minds by the stupid
   behaviour of a miniscule fraction of the student population.
   He directed towards that student minority the sort of
25 veiled threat of financial sanctions best calculated to arouse
   some students to further stupidities. Like ministers in the
   parliamentary debates on immigration, he deliberately met
   the prejudices of the ignorant with a statement calculated
   to exacerbate them.

30   Of course one should be careful about believing that
   Mr Gordon Walker says anything deliberately or with
   calculation. Perhaps he really does not think, as he appears
   to be suggesting, that students should only get their
   (admittedly generous) subsidies on condition that they
35 behave nicely. But Mr Gordon Walker's ineptitudes really
   have grown too numerous. No doubt Mr Wilson is going
   to sack him as soon as a government reshuffle is due. Mean-
   while he is doing harm at a rate scarcely rivalled in recent
   ministerial experience.

   Economist, 16 March 1968

   2 *the Defence Secretary:* the government minister responsible for
   defence.

   10 *Secretary for Education and Science:* the government minister
   responsible for education and science.

16 *students are supported by the taxpayers:* in Britain most students taking a first degree are helped by non-returnable grants of money from their local education authority.

36 *Mr Wilson:* Prime Minister of the British Labour government from 1964 to 1970.

37 *government reshuffle:* changing the posts of a number of ministers in a government.

65

Let me sum up. I've attempted to outline the values of students that cause them to behave and feel the way they do. Many are young, intelligent, sensitive, altruistic individuals with a strong social conscience and a fervent desire to right the ills of society. Academic life can be extremely demanding at a time of rapid, personal change and often social and psychological frustrations are the motives for political activism. But most of it stems from a genuine and deep idealism that could prove invaluable when these people graduate to positions of power.

It is objectionable to stereotype students by irrelevant externals in the way that recent press comment in local and national papers, and correspondence programmes on the radio, have done. Undoubtedly there are irresponsible students and all students should be subject to the same laws as everyone else. Admittedly students do have social obligations to work, they do have privileges – such as influential speakers to talk to them. They should be wary of alienating other sections of the community. They can indulge themselves because they are relatively uncommitted to the *status quo*.

But they are also the keepers of our conscience, renewing society's idealism in a way that only the young can. The ten thousand or so demonstrators in Grosvenor Square represent thousands more. If you complain at their methods, and yet want to stop the war, then get out and do something yourself. These people are tired of bleating, complacent, middle-class apathy.

Before you condemn all students, before you go purple over long hair and weird clothes, examine the deeper reasons for student behaviour and student power. Other-

wise society may pay a high price with a generation of dis-
illusioned intellectuals perhaps driven to political extrem-
ism. For society seems so keen on uniformity. People are
35 so quick to assume that their values are the only ones and
that everyone else ought to conform.

I know life is made easier if the world is presented in
stereotypes. But we must begin to accept that there aren't
just 'goodies' and 'baddies' in the world. People must
40 try to accept a certain relativity of values, must be prepared
to enter other people's frames of reference, and must
endeavour to tolerate differences. Long-haired, bearded
students are not *a priori* hooligans but people with specific
problems and a certain freedom to explore alternatives to
45 conventional conformity. Deploring their behaviour, their
language and their dress is a nonsensical reply to the
contribution they are trying to make to society.

After all, Jesus had long hair too.

Maurice Punch in *New Society*, 28 March 1968

24 *Grosvenor Square:* a square in London where the American
Embassy is situated.

26 *the war:* a reference to the war in Vietnam.

39 '*goodies*' *and* '*baddies*': a children's expression which comes from
films where the characters were either entirely good or entirely bad.

43 *not* a priori *hooligans:* not hooligans just because they have long
hair and beards (*a priori* – from cause to effect, *Latin*).

66

Taurus
1 Sign of the Bull. 21 April–30 May.
An earth sign. Ruling planet – Venus.

How about Taurus?
Shrewd, pleasure-loving, beauty-loving, docile till goaded,
5 uncomplicated, patient, obstinate, courageous, indolent.

Who Should Taurus Marry?
Scorpio? Happy bed-mate, chancy soul-mate.
Aquarius? Too subtle for uncomplicated you.

August Virgo? Run for your life.
September Virgo? This is it! Ideal.

Zodiac He-Celebrity of the Month

Leslie Charteris. Author. Creator of 'The Saint'. Birthday
12 May. Born in Singapore, son of a surgeon of repute.
Learned Chinese and Malay from the native servants
before he could speak English. Has travelled the world; 15
been seaman, barman, blower-up-of-balloons in a fair-
ground – you name it, Leslie's done it. But first and fore-
most he has always been a story-teller. By the age of nine
he was writing his own magazine – also flogging it. It
featured a comic strip done in match-stick figures. Years 20
later, when he wanted a calling-card device for 'The Saint',
he remembered this match-stick figure, added a halo, and
so was born the Saint symbol.

He christened his hero 'Simon Templar' – twenty-
seven, tall, dark, deeply tanned, slim, handsome – which 25
fitted Leslie's own description perfectly at that time; and
the first adventures of The Saint were modelled on his
own experiences. 'I allowed The Saint over the years to
reach thirty-three, and he's stuck at that ever since.' The
Saint has been portrayed by Brian Aherne, Tom Conway, 30
Vincent Price, Barry Sullivan, Louis Hayward, George
Sanders; and, today, Roger Moore.

Our celebrity has deliberately made The Saint his liveli-
hood. In his third novel, *Meet the Tiger*, he introduced
Simon Templar, and immediately saw such possibilities in 35
the character that he decided to concentrate on building
him up. 'It wasn't all that easy,' he said, 'I had a very
thin time for years, that's why I had to take any job that
came along because I had to eat. Eventually I decided to
gamble on America liking The Saint. I landed there with 40
$50 in my pocket.'

The gamble certainly paid off. Since then twenty-five
million Saint books have been sold; and all over the world,
wherever you find TV, there you will find The Saint. The
business acumen of Leslie Charteris, coupled with his im- 45
aginative writing, enables him to live the sort of fairy-tale
existence we authors dream of – luxury homes in Britain and

America, and as much money as he can ever use I
switched to the zodiac before I passed out with bitter envy
50   Leslie admits to being shrewd, pleasure-loving, docile
till goaded, uncomplicated. . . . 'But not patient, Evadne.'
'Are you a beauty-lover?' 'Yes, all my four wives have been
very beautiful.' After a short, stunned pause, I tried again:
'Taurus is indolent, but obviously you are not?'
55   'You're wrong – I'm bone lazy. I'm the cleverest work-
dodger you'll ever meet. Any more questions?' 'Yes – those
four wives you mentioned, were they the zodiac's choice?'
Our celebrity shook his head. . . . 'No, I like Aries wives
best.'

60 **The Month Ahead for the Zodiac**

Aries: a soft-pedal month
Taurus: a go-ahead month
Gemini: a surprising month
Cancer: a static month
65 *Leo:* a tricky month
Virgo: a moving month
Libra: a lucky month
Scorpio: a baffling month
Sagittarius: a get-rich-quick month
70 *Capricorn:* a thrifty month
Aquarius: a 'watch it mate' month
Pisces: an extravagant month

She-Taurus of the Month

Dame Margaret Rutherford.
75 For getting the DBE because she made us laugh. 'To
make them cry is easy – to make them laugh is slavery.'

Reader of the Month

Mr Stanley Holmes. Born Warley, Birmingham, 19 May
1941. A very promising chart – you have a good future.
80 Mr Holmes asks: 'I work in a garage and I'm frustrated
because I long to work on a farm. Shall I ever realize my
ambition?'
My answer: Taurus is an Earth sign, and so has an affinity
with the land; also 1967 looks like being a good year for you.
85 So . . . .

Zodiac Chat-Up

Fascinating fact about the Cuspal Taurean: Born between 19 and 23 April, you will be an Ari-Taur – a borderline case, born on the join of Aries and Taurus; and the odds are you'll be a genius. (Well, if not quite one, you'll get away with an awful lot in highbrow circles.) 90

Our most famous Ari-Taur: Yehudi Menuhin.

Evadne Price in *She*, May 1967

7 *chancy:* uncertain (colloquial).

12 *The Saint:* the hero of a series of crime novels by Leslie Charteris.

19 *flogging:* selling (colloquial).

21 *calling card:* visiting card.

22 *match-stick figure:* drawing of a person or animal simplified by using only straight lines and circles.

42 *paid off:* succeeded (colloquial).

55 *bone lazy:* thoroughly idle.

61 *soft-pedal month:* a time for acting cautiously (colloquial).

71 *'watch it mate':* be careful (slang).

74 *Dame Margaret Rutherford:* a well-known English stage and film actress.

75 *DBE:* (abbreviation for 'Dame of the Order of the British Empire') an honour given to women by the Sovereign, often for public service.

86 *chat-up:* friendly conversation (colloquial).

92 *Yehudi Menuhin:* a famous violinist.

67

Today's Weather

Midnight Forecast

General situation. Thundery trough of low pressure slowly moving over England and Wales. 1

London, S.E. England, E. Anglia, E. Midlands. Coasts and hill fog clearing. Dull, thundery rain at first, sunny intervals, thunderstorms later. Wind between S.E. and N.E. moderate. Warm. Max. 70° F (21° C). 5

Cen. S., S.W., Cen. N. England, W. Midlands, Channel Is, S. Wales. Mainly dull, thundery rain. Moderate N.E. winds. Temperatures little below normal. 55° F (14° C).

E., N.E. England, Borders, Edinburgh, E. Scotland, Aber- 10 *deen area.* Coast and hill fog, mostly lifting. Mainly dull, thundery rain at times. Moderate or fresh N.E. winds 55° F (13° C).

15 *N. Wales, N.W. England, Lake Dist., S. W. Scotland, Glasgow area, N. Ireland.* Mostly cloudy or dull, rain in places. N.W. winds, moderate. 57° F (14° C).

English Channel, Irish Sea. Slight.

Outlook. Rain or thunderstorms, sunny intervals. Near normal temperatures, warmer in S.

Weather Maps, Reports in the *Daily Telegraph*, May 1967

3 *S.:* abbreviation for South.
3 *E.:* abbreviation for East.
5 *N.:* abbreviation for North.
6 *Max.:* shortened form of maximum.
7 *Is.:* shortened form of Islands.
10 *Borders:* the border country between England and Scotland.
14 *W.:* abbreviation for West.
14 *Dist.:* shortened form of District.

68

1 And now I will show you the best way of all.

I may speak in tongues of men or of angels, but if I am without love, I am a sounding gong or a clanging cymbal. I may have the gift of prophecy, and know every hidden
5 truth; I may have faith strong enough to move mountains; but if I have no love, I am nothing. I may dole out all I possess, or even give my body to be burnt, but if I have no love, I am none the better.

Love is patient; love is kind and envies no one. Love is
10 never boastful, nor conceited, nor rude; never selfish, not quick to take offence. Love keeps no score of wrongs; does not gloat over other men's sins, but delights in the truth. There is nothing love cannot face; there is no limit to its faith, its hope and its endurance.

15 Love will never come to an end. Are there prophets? their work will be over. Are there tongues of ecstasy? they will cease. Is there knowledge? it will vanish away; for our knowledge and our prophecy alike are partial, and the

partial vanishes when wholeness comes. When I was a
child, my speech, my outlook and my thought were all   20
childish. When I grew up, I had finished with childish
things. Now we see only puzzling reflections in a mirror,
but then we shall see face to face. My knowledge now is
partial; then it will be whole, like God's knowledge of me.
In a word, there are three things that last for ever: faith,   25
hope and love; but the greatest of them all is love.

First Letter of Paul to the Corinthians xiii, 1–13: *The New
English Bible*

69

. . . and yet shew I unto you a more excellent way.   1

Though I speak with the tongues of men and of angels,
and have not charity, I am become as sounding brass, or a
tinkling cymbal.

And though I have the gift of prophecy, and understand   5
all mysteries, and all knowledge; and though I have all
faith, so that I could remove mountains, and have not
charity, I am nothing.

And though I bestow all my goods to feed the poor, and
though I give my body to be burned, and have not charity,   10
it profiteth me nothing.

Charity suffereth long, and is kind; charity envieth not;
charity vaunteth not itself, is not puffed up,

Doth not behave itself unseemly, seeketh not her own,
is not easily provoked, thinketh no evil;   15

Rejoiceth not in iniquity, but rejoiceth in the truth;

Beareth all things, believeth all things, hopeth all things,
endureth all things.

Charity never faileth: but whether there be prophecies,
they shall fail; whether there be tongues, they shall cease;   20
whether there be knowledge, it shall vanish away.

For we know in part, and we prophesy in part.

But when that which is perfect is come, then that which
is in part shall be done away.

When I was a child, I spoke as a child, I understood as a   25 child, I thought as a child: but when I became a man, I put away childish things.

For now we see through a glass, darkly; but then face to face: now I know in part; but then shall I know even as
30 also I am known.

And now abideth faith, hope, charity, these three; but the greatest of these *is* charity.

First Epistle of Paul to the Corinthians xiii, 1–13: Authorized Version of *The Bible*, 1611

70

1 'Do you ever feel any pain in your back?' this doctor said.

'Pain,' I said, 'pain?' There are times when you've got a pain and you don't know you've got it till it stops, if you
5 see what I mean. Pain's a funny thing. You can have a pain in your heart and it can make you dead sick, but you can have a pain in your back and not know it's there. 'No, I've got no pain,' I said. She went on tapping away at my back. She had quite nice hands, on the stubby side,
10 but they're sensitive. 'Funny,' I said, 'but I believe I've a pain there now. Seems like I just felt it this minute.'

'Where?' she said, ' – there?' She sounded quite pleased.

'A bit over to the left,' I said, 'a bit higher up.' She tapped me a couple more times and I let out a wince.
15 'There!' I said. 'Yes, there,' I said.

'Is it tender?' she said.

'It is when you prod and mess it about,' I said. 'It ain't too bad when it's left alone.'

She came round front and started sounding on my chest.
20 'Do you cough much?' she said.

'I cough of a morning,' I said, 'but then everybody does after that first cigarette.' I find I'm missing her so after that letter I stick it out until the week-end afterwards comes round and then I go and visit her.
25 'Do you bring anything up when you cough?'

'Up? No, not much, just clear my chest, see. Well that's

the point of coughing ain't it, to bring something up and give the tubes a good clearing out.'

'Breathe in deeply again,' she said, 'and hold it this time.' I took a deep breath and held it. Know what? She doesn't want to let me in. I had to knock, of course, because I'd given her my key back. She kept me at the door but little Malcolm was inside and he heard.

'Let it out slowly,' she said. I was nearly bursting so I just blew it out. She was in front of me and it went into her face, so she just put her finger up and put it against my nose and pressed my head to one side.

'What's up?' I said.

'Will you please keep your head turned away from me,' she said, 'as you're breathing out.'

You think you know a woman, but you don't. A man can never know any woman. 'Keep your head turned away from me as you're breathing out!' Not a nice stroke to come out with at a chest clinic.

Bill Naughton: *Alfie* (MacGibbon & Kee, 1966; Panther, 1968)

6 *dead:* very (slang).
43 *not a nice stroke:* not a pleasant thing to do (slang).

71

Two further points may be mentioned next in connexion with our discussion of the phenomena characterizing hypnosis, although they are only indirectly related to this topic. One is the question of whether people can be induced to commit criminal acts under hypnosis; the other how many people are capable of being hypnotized. Both are questions probably more frequently asked than any others in connexion with hypnosis. Taking the question of the production of criminal activity in hypnotized persons first, it may be said that until fairly recently the more sober writers tended to discountenance this possibility. They tended to quote the case of Charcot's young assistant who failed to induce the young hypnotized girl to take off her clothes, and to infer that, quite generally, a suggestion

15　urging a person to act in ways which were very much
counter to his moral and ethical ideas would not be carried
out, but would merely lead to his awakening. There are,
indeed, many observations of this kind to be found in the
experimental literature, and it may be said with a reasonable
20　degree of confidence that in many cases an *explicit suggestion
to do something unethical or immoral will not be carried out
by the subject.*

　More recently, however, a number of experiments
have been conducted to show, first, that this conclusion is
25　not universally true, and secondly, that the whole frame-
work of the type of experiment on which it is based is
much too narrow. One example may suffice to show the
kind of experimentation involved. The experimenter
demonstrated the power of nitric acid to the subject by
30　throwing a penny into it. The penny, of course, was completely disintegrated and the subject began to realize the
tremendous destructive power of nitric acid. While the
subject's view of the bowl of acid was cut off by the experimenter, an assistant substituted for it a like-sized bowl of
35　methylene-blue water, continuously kept boiling by the
presence in it of miniscule droplets of barium peroxide.

　The hypnotized subject was then ordered to throw the
dish of nitric acid (in actual fact, of course, innocuous
water) over the assistant who was present in the same room.
40　Under these conditions it was possible to induce, under
hypnosis, various subjects to throw what they considered to
be an extremely dangerous acid into the face of a human
being. It might be argued that perhaps they had noticed
the difference between the acid and the water. Actually,
45　in this particular experiment, the person in charge made
what he calls 'a most regrettable mistake in technique'
by forgetting to change the nitric acid to the innocuous dish
of water, so that in one case the assistant had real nitric
acid thrown over him.

H. J. Eysenck: *Sense and Nonsense in Psychology* (Penguin
Books, 1957)

　12 *Charcot:* a French psychologist; one of the first doctors to experiment with hypnosis.
　36 *miniscule:* tiny, minute.

72

Conducted by the Old Codgers   1

We Old Pair bet there were plenty of giggles in the wards
of a Midlands hospital when these instructions were sent
round by the 'Old Man'.

Nurse (full name and address supplied) writes from Leices-   5
ter:

   Recently a very modern clinic was opened by the Duke of
Rutland, at the psychiatric hospital where I work. The enclosed
notice was sent round to all wards: 'On this occasion all nurses
must strictly adhere to regulation uniform.   10
   Female nursing staff will wear apron, black shoes and plain
black stockings.
   Male nursing staff will wear black shoes, regulation ties and
collar and white coat.'
   The 'Old Man' as he is affectionately known, is a dear really,   15
but my! if we'd taken his orders literally where would we stand
with the General Nursing Council?

   Reckon the patients would wonder where to stand,
too!
   New Champ. Mr J. Matthews of Old Barnway, Aberga-   20
venny, Mon. writes:

I can beat the 320 ft 1 in cotton reel knitting record hands down.
In the past eighteen months I have done more than 500 yards.
I have made two rugs 24 × 40 in and three smaller ones. I must
admit I may have had more time than the previous champ because   25
I have been on the sick list.

   Nearly a yard a day? Don't believe in wasting time,
do you?
   Mrs M. Jones of Essex Street, Luton, Beds, writes:

My friend has to go to a London hospital for a check-up once or   30
twice a year, so we make it a day out as well, as we are both OAPs.
   We always go by bus to the second stop in the Strand and up a
side street to a pub where we have lunch and a drink. A lot of City
gents like yourselves (I hope) come in, complete with bowler hats
and briefcases.   35
   Well, we had quite a laugh. Two of these gents came in and I

said: 'There's the Old Codgers, only they haven't brought Lottie and George.' Then the door opened and in came a young couple – and the girl called him George!

40 So that's where they sneak off to at lunchtime, the young varmints!

'Live Letters' in the *Daily Mirror*, 1967

1 *Old Codgers:* old fellows (colloquial), used here to represent two imaginary journalists who run a correspondence column.

3 *Midlands:* the counties in the centre of England.

17 *General Nursing Council:* the national nursing organization in Britain concerned with standards of training and conduct in the nursing profession.

20 *champ:* shortened form of champion (colloquial).

22 *hands down:* easily (colloquial).

31 *OAP:* (abbreviation for Old-Age Pensioner) a person who receives a pension from the State.

33 *City gents:* ('gents', shortened form of 'gentlemen') the City is the financial centre of London, and employees of many City firms traditionally wear dark suits and bowler hats.

37 *Lottie and George:* imaginary friends of the Old Codgers.

73

1 *Running-In Speeds*

The treatment given to a new car will have an important bearing on its subsequent life, and engine speeds during this early period must be limited. The following instruc-
5 tions should be strictly adhered to:

During the first 500 miles (800 km.)

Do not exceed 45 m.p.h. (72 km.p.h.).

Do not operate at full throttle in any gear.

Do not allow the engine to labour in any gear.

10 *Starting*

Before starting the engine ensure that the gear lever is in neutral and the hand brake is applied. If the engine is cold pull out the choke control.

Switch on the ignition, ensure that the ignition and oil
15 pressure warning lights glow and that the fuel gauge registers, then operate the starter. Release it if the engine

fails to start within five or six seconds, wait for the crank-shaft to stop rotating, and then turn the key again.

Should the engine not start after a reasonable number of attempts, check for possible causes. Do not persist in using the starter as a great strain is imposed on the battery by so doing.

As soon as the engine starts, release the starter switch and warm up the engine at a fairly fast idling speed. Should the oil-pressure warning light remain on, stop the engine immediately and investigate the cause. Failure to do so may result in serious damage to the engine. Also check that the ignition warning light goes out when the engine is running above idling speed. Failure of the light to behave in this fashion indicates a broken fan belt or other fault in the system. Push in the choke control completely as soon as the engine will run evenly without its use.

Warming-Up

Research has proved that the practice of warming up an engine by allowing it to idle slowly is harmful. The correct procedure is to let the engine run fairly fast, approximately 1000 r.p.m. corresponding to a speed of about 15 m.p.h. (24 km.p.h.) in top gear, so that it attains its correct working temperature *as quickly as possible*. Allowing the engine to work slowly in a cold state leads to excessive cylinder wear, and far less damage is done by driving the car straight on to the road from cold than by letting the engine idle slowly in the garage.

British Motor Corporation: *Driver's Handbook* – Morris 1100

1 *Running-In:* the period when a new car engine is settling down and speeds should be controlled.

7 *m.p.h.:* abbreviation for miles per hour.

11 *the gear lever is in neutral:* a position in which no power is trans-mitted to the engine.

24 *idling speed:* the speed at which a car engine turns when it is not being accelerated.

37 *r.p.m.:* abbreviation for revolutions per minute.

How a Legend Died

1   In chastising his party and publicly humiliating some of
his oldest friends, Mr Wilson, like a sorrowing father, may
have hurt himself more than them. And the pain is likelier
to last.

5   Although by this week-end tempers had cooled and the
shock effects had worn off, most people agreed that relations between the Prime Minister and the Left of the
party, which helped him to power, could never be the same
again.

10   Mr Wilson's performance at the Parliamentary Labour
Party meeting was deliberately low-keyed; even vituper-
ative phrases, likening his critics to vicious dogs, were
pronounced with minimal malice. He afterwards affected
surprise at the fuss; but he must have known he was
15   killing a legend ('the party is a crusade or it is nothing' he
used to say) and replacing it with no more than a brutal
reminder that members owe their living to him.

Ostensibly, the unexpectedly large number of intentional
abstainers last Tuesday (sixty-three say the rebels, forty-
20   eight say the whips) was a once-for-all experience. Many
confessed afterwards they could not see any other cause
than defence on which they could band together. It could
be argued that the bad habit needed to be stopped: 'Absten-
tion is like adultery,' said one young MP. 'The first time
25   is much the hardest.' It is also true that the authorities
might be alarmed by the unpredictable size of the new
grouping.

Ministers at first pooh-poohed the revolt; didn't we
know the party suffered from a spasm like this every year
30   of its life when national defence was debated?

It would have been easy to drop a few hints and let
things be: but the Prime Minister decided the time was
ripe for a brisk intervention. The occasion was good:
rebellions are mostly left-wing, but he could preserve his
35   notorious impartiality by blaming both sides equally.

Nora Beloff in the *Observer*, 5 March 1967

2 *Mr Wilson:* Prime Minister in the British Labour government from 1964 to 1970.

7 *the Left:* the Left Wing, those more in favour of far-reaching reforms than others within the same political party.

10 *Parliamentary Labour Party:* the organization of Labour Members of Parliament in the House of Commons.

20 *the whips:* certain Members of Parliament who have to make sure that others in their party vote on important occasions.

24 *MP:* abbreviation for Member of Parliament.

75

The conquest of England by the Norman invaders brought about an influx of French words which went on increasing in volume for more than three centuries. At first it was little more than a trickle. For a long time the Norman conquerors did not mix much with their Saxon subjects. There are plenty of indications of this; for the languages, too, moved side by side in parallel channels. The custom of having one name for a live beast grazing in the field and another for the same beast, when it is killed and cooked, is often supposed to be due to our English squeamishness and hypocrisy. Whether or not the survival of this custom through ten centuries is due to the national characteristics in question it would be hard to say, but they have certainly nothing to do with its origin. That is a much more blameless affair. For the Saxon neatherd who had spent a hard day tending his *oxen, sheep, calves* and *swine*, probably saw little enough of the *beef, mutton, veal, pork* and *bacon*, which were gobbled at night by his Norman masters. There is something a little pathetic, too, in the thought that the homely old word, *stool*, could be used to express any kind of seat, however magnificent, until it was, so to speak, hustled into the kitchen by the smart French *chair*. Even the polite, however, continued to use the old word in the idiom 'to fall between two stools'.

Owen Barfield: *History in English Words* (Faber, 1954)

1 *Norman:* Normans, or North-men, were the descendants of a Teutonic Danish tribe who had taken possession of Normandy about a hundred and fifty years before their invasion of England in 1066.

5 *Saxon:* a people once living in north-western Germany, some of whom conquered and settled in England in the fifth and sixth centuries.

15 *neatherd:* a boy or man who looks after animals (archaic).

24 '*to fall between two stools*': to fail in something by hesitating between two courses of action.

76

Alien Invaders

Natives Need Not Suffer Guilt Complex

1 Sir,

The bulk of comment on the Political and Economic Planning racial discrimination report puts the British people in the dock. Why? The most natural instinct in a
5 free and homogeneous people – to resist invasion by aliens on their native habitat and way of life – has been castigated as shameful. A generation ago it was lauded as heroic.

It is utterly preposterous to work up a guilt complex in
10 the natives of this country, simply because, for a variety of excellent reasons, they like to employ their own breed in preference to coloured aliens. What right have the latter, who come here voluntarily for their own benefit, to demand acceptance over the natives? And why assume that their
15 rejection is prejudice against them? It might equally be preference for native Britons, and what in heaven's name is wrong with that?

The coloured invasion threatens our whole security. The alien has his foot in our door, and what is glibly condemned
20 as racial discrimination is in fact a perfectly natural and proper desire for self-preservation. It is not the colour of their faces, but their numbers which we dislike.

Discrimination implies choice, and freedom of choice is the very essence of democracy. To extend legislation
25 compelling us to admit coloured aliens to our homes, shops and offices in preference to familiar native faces is to deny freedom of choice. It is dictatorship. It is indeed racial discrimination against the British people, in their own country. Already one maternity hospital is so full of immi-
30 grant women that a British expectant mother, who had

been a nurse there, was at first refused a bed, then given
one in a ward where she was the only British patient.

To the extent that incompatible aliens are 'integrated'
the native Briton will leave. This classic trend is already
appearing. In the September quarter of 1966, 12,000 more   35
people left Britain than arrived here. But the emigrants
were native Britons in the professional–managerial class,
while the immigrants were mostly unskilled coloured aliens.
This trend will accelerate if further moral and legal com-
pulsions are imposed on the British people to accept in-   40
compatibles in their society.... If the business of this
country is to be dictated by poor half-castes waving the
big stick of 'racial discrimination', the minority of coloured
aliens – most immigrants are not even subjects of the
Queen – will soon run our country on their own terms.   45
There is no reason at all why they should be allowed to
do so.

Letter in the *Daily Telegraph*, 24 April 1967

2 *Political and Economic Planning:* a research organization.
4 *dock:* in its legal sense, the enclosure for the prisoner in a criminal
court.

77

Toads

Why should I let the toad *work*   1
　　Squat on my life?
Can't I use my wit as a pitchfork
　　And drive the brute off?

Six days of the week it soils   5
　　With its sickening poison –
Just for paying a few bills!
　　That's out of proportion.

Lots of folks live on their wits:
　　Lecturers, lispers,   10
Losels, loblolly-men, louts –
　　They don't end as paupers.

Lots of folk live up lanes
With a fire in a bucket;
15 Eat windfalls and tinned sardines –
They seem to like it.

Their nippers have got bare feet,
Their unspeakable wives
Are skinny as whippets – and yet
20 No one actually *starves*.

Ah, were I courageous enough
To shout *Stuff your pension!*
But I know, all too well, that's the stuff
That dreams are made on:

25 For something sufficiently toad-like
Squats in me too;
Its hunkers are heavy as hard luck,
And cold as snow,

And will never allow me to blarney
30 My way to getting
The fame and the girl and the money
All at one sitting.

I don't say, one bodies the other
One's spiritual truth;
35 But I do say it's hard to lose either,
When you have both.

Philip Larkin: *The Less Deceived* (Marvell Press, 1958)

11 *losels:* scoundrels (dialect).
11 *loblolly men:* country bumpkins, fools (dialect).
15 *windfalls:* fruit blown off a tree by the wind. Traditionally anyone is entitled to eat windfalls.
22 *Stuff your pension!:* you can keep the pension you were going to give me! (vulgar).
23 *that's the stuff/That dreams are made on:* a reference to Shakespeare's *The Tempest*, Act 4 Scene 1: '. . . we are such stuff/As dreams are made on . . . .'
33 *one bodies the other:* one gives substance to the other.

Vulkan's knee was level with the top of my head. I judged   1
my distance with care. There is a groove in the fibula just
below the knee where the lateral popliteal nerve passes
close against the bone. A sharp blow here paralyses the lower
leg – 'dead man's leg' we called it in the school playground.   5

'They are all falling out,' I shouted suddenly in panic.
'The papers.' Johnny clutched the bottom of the envelope
as I pushed it – and his gun – upwards away from my
cranium. I jabbed at his knee. I hit but not accurately
enough. My head sang like a massed-voice choir as the   10
nasty front edge of the magazine hit the side of my head. I
had already begun to fall back. Again I punched out,
scarcely able to see Vulkan's leg for the bright crimson
pain that sang its song in the empty echo chamber of my
head.   15

I felt him go. He toppled like a felled redwood, the
spilled papers spinning and drifting all around him. The
crash of his body collapsing full-length across the bench
was followed by the clatter of dislodged junk. An insurance
renewal slip fell like a sycamore seed into an open tin of   20
grease. 'I've hurt my back,' he said urgently; but training
won out and the Mauser stayed firmly in his fist. Its
chamfered snout made a little circling motion like a clerk's
pencil just about to write. I waited for the bang.

'I've hurt my back,' he said again. I moved towards   25
him but the foresight made that tiny movement again and
I froze. His leg was crossed under him like a stone figure
on a knight's tomb. I saw the real, ageing man behind the
careless young mask. He twisted his shaken body and, more
slowly than I had ever seen him move before, he eased his   30
feet over the edge of the bench towards the greasy floor.
His voice was a soft growl, 'Es irrt der Mensch, so lang er
strebt.' (Man errs till his strife is ended.)

I watched him with that sort of hypnotic horror that
venomous insects provoke, but between me and Johnnie   35
Vulkan there was no glass. His feet took the weight of his
body and his face took its pain. He groped along the bench
towards me. I moved back. He stepped awkwardly as

though his foot had gone to sleep, his muscles uncoordinated, his face twitching, but the Mauser always steady.
His foot descended gently into the big tin of grease. Vulkan
looked down at it. Now was the time to jump him. 'I've
ruined my suit,' he said. The grease splattered around his
leg and the Oxford made a loud squelching noise inside
the tin. He stood with one hand on the bench, one foot
in the tin of grease and the Mauser pointed at my middle.
'My suit,' he said and he laughed gently, keeping his
mouth wide open, like imbeciles and drunks do, until the
laugh became a gurgle, like soap suds going down a kitchen
sink.

Len Deighton: *Funeral in Berlin* (Cape, 1964; Penguin
Books, 1966)

16 *redwood:* a giant tree found mainly in California.
22 *Mauser:* a German automatic pistol.
23 *chamfered:* a sloping edge.
27 *like a stone figure on a knight's tomb:* tombs in the Middle Ages
often displayed a stone likeness of the dead person.
44 *Oxford:* a style of shoe with laces.

79

Synthetic fun is the heart-shaped tablets that send you
high.
Synthetic fun is the smile on the face of the Holiday
Camp 'Fun people' this Friday as every Friday, as they're
ritually thrown into the blue, blue swimming-pool.
Synthetic fun is the smile on the face of the matadors at
the Bloodless Bullfights in Spain, put on specially for the
British.
Synthetic fun is the golden mile of Blackpool's Illumin-
ations with their giant six-foot-high illuminated dwarfs
and toadstools.
Synthetic fun is the ever-present constant de-sexing,
freezing, pre-packing of experience, so that it may be
daisy-fresh, oven-ready, cellulose-wrapped, and hand-
somely endowed with capsule prizes. Synthetic fun is that
candid look on the face of the nudie, langourous pin-up,

inviting us into her private world with parted lips, gazing into my eyes, offering fulfilment infinite.

Synthetic fun is Soho's new post-Street Offences Act gimmick of kink, titillation, teaze, clip-joints, strip-clubs. 20

Synthetic fun is a million pills swallowed every day, three-quarter million pep pills, two and a half million sleeping pills, with which we drown or titillate our raddled senses. Synthetic fun is the ad-man's dream-world in which he who reads may become once more potent, 25 strong.

Synthetic fun is the handshake of the showman peers as they emerge from among their bison, nudists, autos, pasteboard, to autograph yet one more lavishly illustrated souvenir. 30

Synthetic fun is those evening telly programmes, hotted up from the morning before.

Synthetic fun is the salesman bulging free gifts for the lucky housewife.

Synthetic fun is the disc-jockey's joke as he mouths from 35 his heaving nest in the ocean.

Synthetic fun is the waiter's joke as he greets you to your favourite suite in the Grand Hotel Splendide Imperial Babylon.

Synthetic fun is the glossy array of fictional characters 40 thrown up by our gossip columnists.

Synthetic fun is the smile on the face of the model girl.

Synthetic fun is the smile on the face of the whore.

Synthetic fun is the teenagers shaking, crazy, as if they'd never be old. 45

Synthetic fun is charm schools that teach 'what is and what is not acceptable in the realms of laughter'.

Synthetic fun is 'a nation that, in large degree, when the day's work is done goes home to television'.

Synthetic fun is the sausage-eating competition, organized 50 by the sausage makers.

Synthetic fun is the ritual sitting in a traffic jam for hour after hour somewhere in Somerset on a road whose name is a number.

Synthetic fun is shampooing 'new breathless colour 55 excitement' into your hair.

Jeremy Sandford and Roger Law: *Synthetic Fun* (Penguin Books, 1967)

1 *heart-shaped tablets:* a reference to the slang term, 'purple hearts', for a certain stimulant drug.

1 *send you high:* give you a feeling of elation as a result of taking drugs (slang).

9 *Blackpool:* a well-known holiday resort on the north-west coast o England.

14 *daisy-fresh, oven-ready:* typical advertising terms.

15 *capsule prizes:* 'miniaturized' prizes.

16 *pin-up:* a photograph, usually of a girl, cut out of a magazine or newspaper and pinned up on the wall (colloquial).

19 *post-Street Offences Act:* ('post' – after, *Latin*) the Street Offences Act of 1959 cleared prostitution off the streets.

20 *clip-joints:* night-clubs where customers are often cheated of their money (slang).

22 *pep pills:* mild stimulants (slang).

24 *ad-man:* advertising man; a person who writes and plans for advertising campaigns (slang).

27 *showman peers:* members of the nobility who open their country estates to the public for payment and provide varied entertainment there.

31 *telly:* shortened form of television (colloquial).

35 *disc-jockey:* a radio announcer who introduces and publicizes popular records.

36 *heaving nest:* a reference to the private radio stations – now illegal – on ships anchored off the British coast.

41 *gossip columnists:* most popular daily newspapers run a gossip column.

46 *charm schools:* schools which teach women social graces.

80

1 **If Jaded or Faded** ask superior chemist for *Badedas* (contains mysterious extract of horse-chestnuts). Put it in your bath like all sophisticated Europe. Experience Lebenslust!

5 **Canals in England and Wales.** Explore the romantic past through the peaceful and picturesque waterways of old England and Wales in a traditional narrow boat with all modern conveniences including H & C. Showers and fridge. Send for illustrated brochure stating numbers in

10 party and probable dates to Bradbeer (Dept 5YO), Lowestoft, Suffolk.

Calling all Young Couples, Families and Friends to Bond Beach Club nr Tarragona, Spain. Your own villa from 10s. each day and when desired all the fun of our Bar, Bistro, Swimming Pool, Barbecue and moonlight dancing 15 to Spanish guitarists. Excursions in our minibus to Bullfights, Vineyards and Roman remains. (Inclusive fortnight's holiday with Saturday day-flight £40 11s. 0d.) Write for brochure today. Dept 01, 17 Bolton Street, W1. Tel. HYD 2578. 20

Fash Fab Chelsea Mod (circa 1930) town res of lapsed Anglican Cambridge graduate Fleet St Girl Reporter 'At 15 busy losing one's faith before going to University ... 'fraid the house has been rather roughed about by all my friends abused by Chelsea type of living ... we had a 25 Beat Group in the bedrm.' Clkrm. Drawing rm. Parquet Dining rm/Study, drs. to Patio. 3 Bedrms (one leads to sunbathing roof terrace – the 3rd is minute, 'But has a human being sleeping in it'). Tiled Bathrm. Kit. Sacrifice £12,995 Freehold – even try offer. View Sun. KEN 8671. 30

Personal and House Advertisements in the *Observer*, 1969

4 *Lebenslust:* delight in life (*German*).

8 *H & C:* abbreviation for 'hot and cold running water'.

15 *Bistro:* an informal French-style restaurant (*French*).

21 *fash, fab, mod:* shortened forms of 'fashionable', 'fabulous' and 'modern' (slang).

21 *Chelsea:* a fashionable district in London, formerly a popular quarter for artists.

21 *res:* shortened form of 'residence' used by house agents.

21 *lapsed Anglican:* a person who has left the Church of England.

22 *Fleet St:* Fleet Street, a street in London famous as the centre of the British newspaper industry.

26 *Beat Group:* a group playing popular music.

26 *Bedrm, Clkrm, Drawing rm:* shortened forms of 'bedroom', 'cloakroom' and 'drawing room' used by house agents.

29 *Kit:* shortened form of 'kitchen' used by house agents.

30 *Sun:* shortened form of 'Sunday'.

1   CALLIPERS, calipers. An instrument for measuring the distance between two points, especially on a curved surface; e.g. for measuring the internal and external diameters of tubes.

5   CALOMEL. See *mercurous chloride*.

CALORESCENCE. Absorption of *light* radiations by a surface, their conversion into *heat*, and the consequent emission of heat *radiation*.

CALORIE. Unit of quantity of *heat*. The amount of heat
10 required to raise the *temperature* of 1 g of *water* through 1° C. The 15° calorie is defined as the amount of heat required to raise the temperature of 1 g of water from 14·5° C to 15·5° C. This calorie is equal to 4·1855 *joules*. The International Table calorie is defined as 4·1868 joules.
15 The joule is the *SI unit* of *heat*.

CALORIE, LARGE. Kilogramme-calorie. 1000 *calories* (q.v.). Written Calorie. Used for quoting energy values of foods.

CALORIFIC VALUE of a fuel. The quantity of *heat* produced
20 by a given weight of the *fuel* on complete *combustion*. Usually given as the number of *British Thermal Units* (q.v.) evolved by the complete combustion of 1 lb of the fuel or in *SI units* in *joules* per *kilogram*. Determined by the *bomb calorimeter* (q.v.).

25 CALORIMETER. Instrument for determining quantities of *heat* evolved, absorbed or transferred. In its simplest form consists of an open cylindrical vessel of copper or other substance of known specific heat (see *heat, specific*).

CALX. 1. The powdery *oxide* of a *metal* formed when an *ore*
30 or a mineral is roasted. 2. Quicklime (see *calcium oxide*).

CAMERA, PHOTOGRAPHIC. A device for obtaining photographs or exposing cinematic film, either coloured or black and white. A camera consists essentially of a *light*-proof box with a *lens* at one end and a light-sensitive film or
35 plate at the other. An 'exposure' is made by opening a 'shutter' over the lens for a predetermined period during which an image of the object to be photographed is thrown upon the light-sensitive film. Focusing is carried out by

varying the distance of the lens from the film by a suitable
device. The amount of light which enters the camera in   40
order to obtain a correctly exposed photograph is determined by the amount of light available (either sunlight or
artificial light), the 'speed' of the film, the *aperture* of the lens
(see *f-number*), and the shutter speed. In the simplest cameras
the shutter speed and aperture are fixed, so that satis-   45
factory photographs can only be obtained in bright sunlight.
In more expensive cameras the aperture can be controlled
by a variable *iris* and several separate shutter speeds are
provided. In some modern cameras the iris is controlled
by the current from a built-in *photo-electric cell* (*exposure*   50
meter) which measures the light available. Thus for given
film and shutter speeds the camera automatically takes a
correctly exposed photograph. In cinematic cameras the
opening of the shutter is mechanically synchronized with
the passage of the film through the camera so that, at   55
normal speeds, between 16 and 24 frames are exposed
every second. See also *photography*.

CAMERA, TELEVISION. That part of a *television* system
which converts optical images into electrical signals. Consists of an optical *lens* system similar to that used in a   60
photographic *camera*, the image from which is projected
into a 'camera tube'. The camera tube comprises a *photo-*
sensitive mosaic which is scanned by an *electron* beam housed
in an evacuated glass tube. The output signals of the
camera tube are usually pre-amplified within the body of   65
the camera.

CAMPHOR. $C_{10}H_{16}O$. A white crystalline *solid* with a characteristic smell, m.p. 178° C. Occurs in the camphor tree.
Used in the manufacture of *celluloid* (q.v.) and in other
industries.   70

E. B. Uvarov, D. R. Chapman and Alan Isaacs: *A Dictionary
of Science* (Penguin Books, revised edition, 1971)

10 *g*: abbreviation for 'gramme.

17 *q.v.*: (abbreviation for 'quod vide', *Latin*), used after a word within a definition (particularly in a dictionary) to direct the reader to a
description of that particular word somewhere else in the book.

68 *m.p.*: melting point.

The State of the Nation

1 No doubt the xenophobia which lay below the surface of
British life during the Sixties and Seventies, and became
explicit in the form of anti-Americanism, was powerfully
exacerbated by the psychological repressions which we
5 shared with other advanced industrial societies. Increased
leisure and the lack of outlet for violent instincts in modern
urban life made for an aimless type of violence among
teenagers which aroused emotional sympathy among
intellectuals. Violence and brutality had been the for-
10 bidden fruit of a humanitarian society, and in the Sixties,
writers and artists began increasingly to react against the
gentleness of British life and to side with what they admired
as the 'creative ruthlessness' of the younger generation.
Later, however, a reaction set in. The systematic beating-up
15 of retirement pensioners which swept through the larger
towns in the early Seventies to the cry of 'scrap the oldies',
and was only stamped out when troops were drafted to aid
the police, gave a shock to those for whom 'youth' could
do no wrong. Discipline in the schools and universities was
20 tightened up, the police were given wider powers, and a
number of parents were made to pay fines running into
hundreds of pounds. Puritanism was not dead after all.
The less permissive atmosphere of the Seventies corres-
ponded to a change in generations. In the decade following
25 1970 teenagers and people in their early twenties began to
display some of the characteristics of the nineteenth-century
Englishman. The emphasis now was on work and self-
reliance. It was no longer thought wrong to make profits –
indeed, there was a scorn for the weak and unenterprising
30 (the complement of which were the outrages against
pensioners). Ten years ago, the wheel had turned full
circle: humanitarianism was again the fashion, unaccom-
panied this time by any very fierce revolt against existing
social values. By now young people are fairly well adapted
35 to society. They are industrious and kindly, intelligent and

unoriginal. Those of them who continue to live for kicks have for the most part ceased to get them by kicking other people.

Anthony Hartley and John Maddox: '1990' in the *Daily Telegraph* Supplement, 3 March 1967

1 *xenophobia:* hatred of foreigners.
36 *to live for kicks:* to live for thrills (slang).

Acknowledgements

For permission to use copyright material acknowledgement is made to the following:

For a letter to the Editor to the *Observer*; for the extract from *This Slimming Business* by John Yudkin to MacGibbon & Kee Ltd; for the article '£338,000. He's Still Only Old Percy' by Len Adams to the *People*; for the extract from *The Cricket in Times Square* by George Selden to J. M. Dent & Sons Ltd; for the article 'José Must Wait for Winstone' by Peter Wilson to the *Daily Mirror*; for the extract from *The Masters* by C. P. Snow to Macmillan and Co. Ltd; for the extract from 'How The Poor Die' from *Shooting an Elephant* by George Orwell to Miss Sonia Brownell and Secker & Warburg Ltd; for the advertisement for Assistant Postal Controllers: Crown Copyright, by courtesy of the Post Office; for the article 'United Sweep to their Title' by Bob Ferrier to the *Observer*; for the advertisement for ceramic tiles to the British Ceramic Tile Council; for the poem 'Attack on the Ad-Man' by A. S. J. Tessimond to Hubert Nicholson, Literary Executor to the late A. S. J. Tessimond; for the extract from *Horse Under Water* by Len Deighton to Jonathan Cape Ltd; for the extract from 'Briefing' to the *Observer*; for the extract from 'Dialling Instructions and Call Charges': Crown Copyright, by courtesy of the Post Office; for the extract from the 'May I Help You?' page by Clare Shepherd to *Woman's Realm*; for the extract from *Kiss Kiss* by Roald Dahl to Michael Joseph Ltd; for the extracts from material for a book on illegitimacy by Marjorie P. Schofield to Anthony Sheil Associates Ltd; for the article on 'Pop Culture' by Edward Lucie-Smith to *The Times*; for the extract from *Room at the Top* by John Braine to Eyre & Spottiswoode Ltd; for the article 'Cliff: The Star with no Escape' by Michael Hellicar to the *Daily Mirror*; for the extract from *Techniques of Persuasion* by J. A. C. Brown to Hedy Brown, executrix of the late J. A. C. Brown; for the article 'MPs Squabble over War Toys' by Hugh Noyes to *The Times*; for the article 'Ban War Toys, says Mrs Kerr' to the *Morning Star*; for the article 'Penalty Area' in Alistair Cooke's America' to the *Guardian*; for the two recipes to Vera Levine; for the article 'The Magic Charles Clore . . . That Was' by Anthony Bambridge to the *Observer*; for a letter to the Editor to the *Observer*; for the extract from *Catch-22* by Joseph Heller to Jonathan Cape Ltd; for the article on the Albert Hall to the *Observer*; for the television programmes to the *Daily Telegraph*; for the article from the *Huddersfield Weekly Examiner* to the Huddersfield Examiner; for the extract from *The Boundaries of Science* by Magnus Pyke to George G. Harrap & Co. Ltd; for the article 'The Competitions Business' by John Barr to *New Society*; for the extract from *Uses and Abuses of Psychology* by H. J. Eysenck to Penguin Books Ltd; for the extract from the poem 'England Expects' from *The Face is Familiar* by Ogden Nash to J. M. Dent & Sons Ltd; for the extract from *How to be an Alien* by George Mikes to André Deutsch Ltd; for the extract from *The American Way of Death* by Jessica Mitford to the Hutchinson Publishing Group Ltd; for the extract from *Roots* by Arnold Wesker to Jonathan Cape Ltd; for the extract from *Our Man in Havana* by Graham Greene to William Heinemann Ltd and The Bodley Head Ltd; for the extract from the article 'Why Children Don't Understand their Parents' by Michael Wynn-Jones to *Nova*; for the extract from *The Blackboard Jungle* by Evan Hunter to Constable & Co. Ltd; for the advertisement for the Salvation Army to Peter Ferguson and the Salvation Army; for the extract from *Hons and Rebels* by Jessica Mitford to Victor Gollancz Ltd; for an extract from 'Briefing' to the *Observer*; for the directions for *Polyfilla* to Polycell Products Ltd; for the article on advertising by Bob Wynn to the *Morning Star*; for the extract from *The Highway Code* to the Controller of Her Majesty's Stationery Office; for the article 'Billy Graham's Advice to UN' by Mary Holland to the *Observer*; for the extract from *Free Fall* by William Golding to Faber & Faber Ltd; for the extract from the National Union of Teachers leaflet to Sir Ronald Gould; for the article by Patrick O'Donovan to the *Observer*; for the extract from *The Fire Next Time* by James Baldwin to Michael Joseph Ltd; for the extract from *Leave Me Alone* by David Karp to Victor Gollancz Ltd; for the extract from *Hansard*: Crown Copyright; for the extract from *Absolute Beginners* by Colin MacInnes to MacGibbon & Kee Ltd; for the extract from the Official Guide to Caernarvon Castle to the Controller of Her Majesty's Stationery Office; for the cover note for the Elgar Violin Concerto (ALP 1456) to EMI Records; for the extract from a company report to The Metal Box Co. Ltd; for the advertisements from the Personal Column to the *Observer*; for the extract from *The Complete Plain Words* by Ernest Gowers to the Controller of Her Majesty's Stationery Office; for the extract from *Suddenly Last Summer* from *Five Plays* by Tennessee Williams to

Secker & Warburg Ltd; for the article on the Nawab of Pataudi by Christopher Ford to the *Guardian*; for the extract from *Chance, Skill and Luck* by John Cohen to Penguin Books Ltd; for the article 'Misplaced Minister' to the *Economist*; for the extract from the article 'Students: Society's Conscience' by Maurice Punch to *New Society*; for the horoscope to Miss Evadne Price and *She*; for the weather forecast to the *Daily Telegraph*; for the extract from *The New English Bible*, New Testament, to the Oxford and Cambridge University Presses; for the extract from the Authorized Version of *The Bible*: Crown Copyright; for the extract from *Alfie* by Bill Naughton to MacGibbon & Kee Ltd; for the extract from *Sense and Nonsense in Psychology* by H. J. Eysenck to the author; for the 'Live Letters' to the *Daily Mirror*; for the extract from the Morris 1100 *Driver's Handbook* to British Leyland (Austin-Morris) Ltd; for the article on Harold Wilson by Nora Beloff to the *Observer*; for the extract from *History in English Words* by Owen Barfield to Faber & Faber Ltd; for a letter to the Editor to the *Daily Telegraph*; for the poem 'Toads' from *The Less Deceived* by Philip Larkin to The Marvell Press; for the extract from *Funeral in Berlin* by Len Deighton to Jonathan Cape Ltd; for the extract from *Synthetic Fun* by Jeremy Sandford and Roger Law to Penguin Books Ltd; for the personal and house advertisements to the *Observer*; for the extract from *A Dictionary of Science* (Revised Edition) by E. B. Uvarov, D. R. Chapman and Alan Isaacs to Penguin Books Ltd; for the article 'The State of the Nation' by Anthony Hartley and John Maddox to the *Daily Telegraph*.

Author and Source Index

The number refers to the passage

Subject Index

The number refers to the passage

Success with English
General Editor: Geoffrey Broughton
Lecturer in English as a Foreign Language,
University of London Institute of Education

A completely new and fully integrated approach in three
stages to the teaching of English as a foreign language to
adult students or the upper forms of secondary schools. With
this carefully planned scheme it has been possible to provide
training in every kind of language skill – reading, writing and,
above all, talking and listening in realistic situations.

The emphasis throughout is on English as it is spoken today,
the English people use and need, the English of shops and
libraries, parties and the cinema, letters and telephones. The
approach is entirely situational: language is taught and
practised without recourse to descriptive or legislative grammar.

The course is also exceptionally flexible. It can be used in
both foreign and second language territories, with large or
small classes, or by the self-help student. Similarly, the speed
at which the course is worked is not critical.

Outlook: Science at Work
Outlook: Artists Talking

Two fully illustrated readers which offer a lively, open-minded
and up-to-date look at the way things are going in applied
sciences and the arts. There are no notes provided as the
texts have been edited with the intention of encouraging
inference of meaning from the context and illustrations, and
the use of a dictionary. These readers are designed to
accompany Stage 2 of *Success with English*, though they can
also be used quite independently of the course.

Outlook: Science at Work
John Parry

Would you live in a city at sea? Or in a climate controlled by
infra-red rays? What would it be like to videophone someone
instead of telephoning them?
Outlook: Science at Work looks at where technology has got to
and where it is going. Simply and clearly, with many diagrams
and photographs, it explains the latest developments and what
they are likely to mean to the world we live in.

Over 50 diagrams and photographs

Outlook: Artists Talking
Five Artists Talk to Anthony Schooling

Five artists working in Britain today – all of them important
innovators in their field – talk to Anthony Schooling on topics
which range from government help for the arts to fashion in
Britain. A film and stage director, a novelist, an architect,
a painter and a fashion designer all talk informally, but
seriously, about their work, their ambitions, their lives and the
society around them.

Edited from the original transcripts of the interviews, *Outlook:
Artists Talking* provides lively reading practice in authentic
contemporary English conversation.

Lavishly illustrated with photographs

WEST WYTHENSHAWE
COLLEGE of FE
Moor Road
Wythenshawe Manchester M23 9BQ